Anonymous

Guide to Florida

Anonymous

Guide to Florida

ISBN/EAN: 9783337112783

Printed in Europe, USA, Canada, Australia, Japan

Cover: Foto ©Andreas Hilbeck / pixelio.de

More available books at **www.hansebooks.com**

GUIDE TO FLORIDA.

FLORIDA—ITS DISCOVERY.

HAD Christopher Columbus, on leaving the Island of San Salvador, proceeded Westward, he would have ultimately discovered the coast of Florida; for the Gulf Stream, then an unknown power, would have swept him to the Northward—the difference of Latitude required for the purpose. But, influenced by the description of the natives, of a land of wealth bearing to the southward, he directed his prow thither, and brought up on the coast Cuba. Thus was reserved to one of Columbus' companions, (Juan Ponce de Leon,) the honor of the discovery of the peninsula; a most romantic incident of History.

In 1512, the brave old soldier, Ponce de

Leon, was Governor of Porto Rico. He had carved his way to glory and wealth, but nevertheless aspired to equal Columbus in renown, and for that purpose fitted out an expedition.

It was whilst discussing the subject with his followers, and arguing as to the course to be pursued, that an Indian Cacique narrated to them a wonderful story; that, not many leagues away, towards the setting sun, there existed a land of great riches, and exceeding all others in beauty of scenery. But, what was most extraordinary, it possessed a marvellous fountain, whose waters had the power to renew youth and give vigor to those who bathed in or drank them.

Ponce de Leon had witnessed such wonderful things in his several voyages, that he was prepared to give credence to the most exagerated accounts.

" What if it should prove true?" soliloquized the old warrior, as he listened to the interpreter.

"And why should it not be? Have I not already discovered marvels, which in my youthful days I would have deemed impossible as this? Ponce de Leon will, in giving to the world a rejuvenating fountain, be entitled to greater renown than those who merely gave wealth and continents to their sovereigns."

An expedition of three vessels was immediately fitted out and set sail from St. Germain, Porto Rico, in March 1512. Ponce de Leon directed its course to the Bahamas. He visited the various localities where the fountain might be, but his search proved fruitless. Island after island was explored, and the waters tasted and bathed in, yet the desired effect was not produced. Nothing daunted, the brave soldier steered to the Westward; and, on Palm Sunday, the Pascua Florida of the Spaniards, (27th March, 1512) he discovered land ahead—a land of such magnificent vegetation and variety of flowers, that he gave to it the name it continues to bear—Florida.

On April 2, 1512, Ponce de Leon disembarked a little to the northward of St. Augustine, planted a cross, and took possession of the country in the name of his sovereign. He then turned his attention to the search for the

"Fountain of Youth;" and, in its absence, gold and precious stones. He found neither, and two months later returned to Porto Rico.

In spite of his want of success, De Leon made a brilliant report of the value of his discovery, and was rewarded by the Crown with the title of Adelentado, or Governor of Florida; in return for which he agreed to conquer and colonize it. This, however, he did not appear in any particular hurry to do; as it was not until nearly ten years later that he again set out for the peninsula.

In the meantime, several explorers had visited its shores and described it as a vast continent, and not an Island as he supposed it to be. At this time, Cortez was in Mexico; and the reports of his conquests and spoils incited Ponce de Leon to put on foot a second expedition, in the hope of meeting with a like success. He sailed, therefore, with two vessels; but no sooner had he landed in Florida, than he was attacked by the natives with such fierceness that, after a severe conflict, the Spaniards were compelled to re-embark and return to Cuba. Ponce himself received a wound, from the effects of which he died, soon after reaching the Island. His epitaph was: "In this sepulchre rest the bones of a man who was a Lion by name, and still more by nature."

DE AYLLON—NARVAEZ—NUNEZ DE VACA.

SHORTLY after the death of Ponce de Leon, Diego Miruelo, the captain of a small Spanish vessel, being driven by stress of weather to the coast of Florida, received from the natives, in traffic, a quantity of gold and silver. With these he returned to St. Domingo; and the accounts he gave of the country he had visited caused much excitement on the Island. At that time there was, in St. Domingo, a company engaged in gold mining, at whose head was a distinguished young nobleman named Lucas Vasquez de Ayllon. This gentleman, as will be seen, was possessed of keenness and a daring spirit.

De Ayllon, fearing, no doubt, his annual statement for the year 1521, would make but a sorry figure, owing to the scarcity of labor on the Island, determined to visit the mainland, and secure a couple of cargoes of the savages so plausibly described by Miruelo.

Now, owing to the efforts of Las Casas, the Spanish crown had prohibited the enslaving of the natives of the New World. This prohibition, however, did not include the Caribs, who were said to be cannibals. De Ayllon, consequently, gave out that the two vessels he was fitting out were for the purpose of obtaining Caribs; but, sailing directly to the mainland, he was driven by stress of weather and the unknown currents further to the north than he anticipated, and came to anchor on the coast of what is now South Carolina, at a place called Chicora, but which he named St. Helena.

Here the Indians at first fled in terror at the sight of ships and white men, whom they beheld for the first time; but the Spaniards soon quieted their fears; and they returned, bringing presents of furs, pearls, and small quantities of gold and silver. The Spaniards gave them trinkets in return, and invited them on board their vessels, to which the confiding natives repaired in considerable numbers. Securing them below the hatches, the Spaniards weighed anchor and set sail for home. One of the vessels foundered at sea, and of the poor captives confined on board of the other, the ancient historian says: "these Indians profited them nothing, for they all died of care and grief."

De Ayllon shortly afterwards obtained from his sovereign the appointment of Governor of Chicora; he fitted out an expedition of three vessels to conquer his new dominion, landing near St. Helena. The inhabitants received him with apparent cordiality; but, after feasting his soldiers for three days, they rose upon them in the night and massacred almost the entire force; including De Ayllon himself.

DE NARVAEZ—1528.

THE next expedition to Florida was conducted on a grander scale; it was led by Pamphilo de Narvaez. De Narvaez, who was a distinguished soldier, had been sent by Velasquez, the Governor of Cuba, to Mexico, with nearly two thousand troops to supersede Cortez, whose brilliant career had excited the jealousy of the Governor. Instead of turning over the command of his three hundred warriors to Narvaez, Cortez, at night, fell upon his rival; and, after a short struggle, in which Narvaez lost an eye, took him prisoner. Then almost the whole of the new comers went over to Cortez.

When, subsequently, Narvaez proceeded to Spain, he was consoled by having conferred upon him the Governorship of Florida. He immediately fitted out an expedition of five vessels; and, on April 12th, 1528, landed on the west coast of Florida, near what is now called Tampa Bay. There he landed three hundred men and forty-five horses. Against the advice of some of his followers, Narvaez determined to at once penetrate the country in search of an empire which should rival Mexico or Peru. His companions had counselled their remaining by their ships, and coasting along the continent; but Narvaez was not to be moved; and, after instructing his captains to take the vessels to some convenient harbor to await his arrival, he started on his march, in a northerly direction.

Instead of finding the rich country they had fancied, the Spaniards could scarcely scrape the wherewith sufficient to keep body and soul together; whilst the natives, differing totally from those of Mexico, contested every inch of ground, with a desperation that discouraged and astonished the Spaniards. History offers few such records of suffering as is narrated in the pages which describe the march of Narvaez through Florida. Narvaez found nothing but swamps and starvation, with hostile Indians on every hand. After losing a large number of his force by sickness and the arrows of the natives, Narvaez, in despair, called a council of his officers.

His hopes of wealth and conquest were at an end;· he sought how best to escape from the country before they should all perish. Irving says: "To proceed along the coast in search of the fleet, or to retrace their steps, would be to hazard the lives of all. At length it was suggested that they should construct small barks, launch them upon the deep, and keep along the coast until they should find their ships. It was a forlorn hope, but they caught at it like drowning men. They accordingly set to work with great eagerness; One of them constructed a pair of bellows out of deer skins, furnishing it with a wooden pipe. Others made charcoal and a forge. By the aid of these, they soon turned their stirrups, spurs, crossbows, and other articles of iron, into nails, saws, and hatchets. The tails and manes of the horses, twisted with the fibres of the palm-treee, served for rigging; their shirts, cut open and sewed together, furnished sails; the fibrous part of the palm-tree also was used as oakum; the resin of the pine trees for tar; the skins of horses were made into vessels to contain fresh water; and a quantity of maize was secured, after hard fighting with the neighboring natives. A horse was killed every three days for provisions for the laboring hands and the sick."

Having at length, by great exertions, completed five frail barks, on the 22d of September they embarked from forty to fifty persons in each; but they were so closely crowded that there was scarcely room to move, while the gunwales of the boats were pressed down to the water's edge. Setting sail from this bay, which they called the Bay of Caballos, they proceeded on, for several days, to an island, where they secured five canoes, which had been deserted by the Indians. These having been attached to their barks enabled them to sail with greater comfort. They passed through the strait between the island and the mainland, which they called the Strait of San Miguel, and sailed onward, for many days enduring the torments of hunger and parching thirst. The skins which contained their fresh water having burst, several men, driven to desperation, drank salt water and died miserably. Their sufferings were aggravated by a fearful storm.

At length they approached "a more populous and fertile part of the coast," upon which they landed, occasionally, to procure provisions; and were immediately involved in bloody affrays with the natives. Thus harassed by sea and land, famishing with hunger, their barks shattered and scarcely manageable, these unfortunate wanderers lost all presence of mind, and became wild and desperate. They were again driven out seaward, and scattered during a stormy night.

At daybreak three of the tempest-tossed barks rejoined each other. In the best-manned and fastest sailer, was Pamphilo de Narvaez. Alvar Nunez, who had command of another boat, seeing the Adelantado making for the land, appealed to him for aid; but Narvaez replied, "that it was no longer time to help others, but that every one must take care of himself." He then steered for the land, abandoning Alvar Nunez to his fate.

After sailing along the coast for many days, Narvaez anchored one night off the land. His crew, with but two exceptions, had repaired on shore, in search of provisions. These two were a sailor and a page who were sick. In the meantime, a violent northerly gale sprung up; and the boats, in which was neither food nor water, were driven to sea. They were never heard of afterward, and thus ended the ill-fated expedition of Pamphilo de Narvaez.

Narvaez had embarked at a point near Apalachicola Bay, and set out in his frail vessels to reach the Spanish Settlements in Mexico, under the impression derived from the charts of the day, that these were nearer to him than the shores of Cuba. The truth, however, was, that the latter were scarcely four hundred miles distant, whilst the nearest Spanish settlement was eleven hundred miles away. This error doubtless cost him his life. At the time of his death, there remained alive about one hundred of his followers, but they gradually separated; and, through hunger and the arrows of the natives, were reduced to four persons—Cabeça de Vaca, Treasurer; Captain Alonzo Castillo; Captain Andreas Dorantes; and Estevanico, an Arabian Negro or Moor. These owed their safety to their being considered by the Indians great medicine-men. De Vaca, according to an account which he published on reaching Spain, had performed some remarkable cures, which he acknowledged surprised himself.

Having spent six years with the tribe he designates as the Mariannes, De Vaca and his three companions, by that time fully conversant with the language and customs of the Indians, set forth to attempt the task of reaching the Settlements in Mexico. Their experience in the healing art did them good service, for by it they were enabled to pass through the many tribes who occupied the shores of the Gulf of Mexico. They crossed the Mississippi, and at length reached, in safety, Mexico, from whence he returned to Spain, where he published the interesting account of his adventures. De Vaca was the first white man who traversed the Cotton States; and to him belongs the credit of the discovery of the Mississippi, and not to De Soto. Narvaez's fleet searched for the Governor during the space of a year, and then returned to Cuba.

HERNANDO DE SOTO.

ONE would have thought that the sad fate of Narvaez would have deterred further expeditions to Florida; but such was not the case, and the story of the adventures of De Vaca, fraught with sufferings, seemed only to stimulate the adventurous spirit of the day. It was not the aspiration to glory, but the greediness of wealth which inspired those adventurers. They believed in a continent exceeding Mexico or Peru in precious metals, and therefore sought it. When Hernando de Soto, the companion of Pizarro, announced his intention of fitting out an expedition, thousands flocked to his standard.

Hernando de Soto belonged to one of the noblest families of Spain; he was born in 1501. At an early age, having, as an old Chronicler says, but his sword for his estate, he joined D'Avilas, who had been made Governor of the West Indies. De Soto found favor in the eyes of the latter, and, in 1531, was given command of a body of men, with whom he joined Pizarro, then on his way to the conquest of Peru. Pizarro soon recognized in De Soto a leading spirit; he made him second in command. Uniting prudence to valor he was ever foremost in every struggle, and invariably victorious.

De Soto had the good fortune to capture the Inca, and to put to flight his forces. The conquest of Peru achieved, Pizarro would have retained De Soto with him, but the latter determined to return to Spain. This he did in 1536, carrying with him, as his share of the spoils of the Inca, 180,000 crowns of gold. He appeared at the court of Charles V., surrounded by a splendid retinue, creating a sensation which made him the lion of the hour. His influence at court increased, and was strengthened by his marriage with Isabella de Bobadilla, daughter of De Aviles, one of the most powerful families of the kingdom.

It was about that time that De Vaca brought to Spain the tidings of the fate of Narvaez. De Soto sought De Vaca; and, after listening to his narrative, hastened to the Emperor, and offered to conquer Florida at his own expense. His Majesty was graciously pleased to grant the request, and conferred upon him the title of Adelantado, in addition to that of Governor of Florida and Cuba for life. As we have already said, no sooner was it known that De Soto was fitting out an expedition, than thousands flocked to his standard; but he chose only the young and vigorous, such as could best endure the hardships and dangers of the expedition.

On April 6, 1538, De Soto sailed with a fleet of ten vessels. His force consisted of a thousand men, commanded by the élite of the Spanish cavaliers. In the largest vessel, the "San Cristoval," a ship of eight hundred tons, was the Governor, his wife Doña Isabel, and his family and retinue. The fleet touched the Canary Islands and reached Santiago de Cuba in May.

De Soto remained in Cuba a year, acclimating his forces and obtaining information as to the Continent he was about to visit. Indian guides from the Florida Coast were obtained, and every precaution taken to ensure the success of the enterprise. All being in readiness, the expedition started in May, 1539; and, on the 25th of the same month, disembarked its thousand men and 350 horses at Tampa Bay. De Soto remained awhile in the vicinity of his landing, endeavoring to conciliate Hirrituqua, the powerful Cacique of the neighborhood. His efforts proved vain—the Chief was obdurate. This can be readily understood when we know that Narvaez, in a transport of rage, for a trivial cause, had ordered the Cacique's nose to be cut off and his mother to be torn by dogs.

Whilst attempting to negotiate with the Chief, De Soto learned that a follower of Narvaez was living with a neighboring tribe, whose chief was named Mucoso. He was greatly pleased with the news, as he fully appreciated the importance to the expedition of having as guide one who had been living in the country ten years, and who was doubtless familiar with the language and customs of the natives. De Soto at once set about securing the person of Juan Ortiz—such was the Spaniard's name; he accordingly despatched his trusty lieutenant, De Gallegos, with a company of lancers, under the guidance of an Indian, on an embassy to the Cacique Mucoso, soliciting the release of Ortiz, and inviting the Chief to his camp, with promises of friendship and munificent rewards.

In the meantime, Mucoso, learning of De Soto's arrival in the neighboring province and fearing that it was his intention to conquer the whole country, despatched Ortiz on a mission to the Governor to pray De Soto not to lay waste his whole territory, and that in return he and his people would be devoted to his service. Ortiz, highly pleased with his mission, set out, accompanied by a body of chosen warriors. They had proceeded but a short distance, when, at the edge of a forest, they suddenly came upon Gallegos and his lancers—the companions of Ortiz retreating to the woods; but Ortiz, forgetting that, with quiver at back, a bow and arrow in hand, and his head adorned with feathers, he differed but little from his companions, scorned the advice, and marched forth to meet his countrymen, who, he thought, would recognize him. The Spaniards, seeing the Indians, at once charged upon them, driving them to the woods, leaving one dead upon the field. Ortiz was nearly ridden over by a trooper—he cried out lustily, "Seville," at the same time making the sign of the cross. The Spaniard reined in his horse, and learning he had found the object of their search, seized

Ortiz by the arm, lifting him upon the croup of his saddle, and dashed off with him to Gallegos, who returned to De Soto in great glee with his prize. The Governor received Ortiz in the warmest manner, sympathized with his past sufferings, and at once ordered him arms, clothing, and a horse.

Ortiz narrated his experience to De Soto; it was most romantic. It appeared that Narvaez, upon landing in Florida, sent back to Cuba, with despatches, one of his smallest vessels, upon which was Juan Ortiz—she immediately returned laden with supplies for the forces; but by that time Narvaez had marched into the interior. The Spaniards, from their vessel, saw on shore some Indians, who pointed to a letter in the end of a cleft stick fixed in the earth. Believing it to contain instructions from Narvaez, they made signs to the Indians to bring it to them, but this they declined to do.

Juan Ortiz and three companions then went to the shore in a boat; but were no sooner landed than they were in a moment surrounded and hastened away. The crew of the vessel, alarmed at the treatment of their shipmates, and the number of the enemy in sight, set sail, leaving Ortiz and his companions to their fate. By this decoy, the Indians secured the captives required to gratify the Cacique's revenge upon the Spaniards, for Hirritriqua was smarting under the loss of his nose, and was overjoyed when the prisoners were brought before him. They were placed under a strong guard until a festival day, when one by one they were made to run the gauntlet, and in this way three of them perished miserably. Ortiz had been reserved for the last; and the chief, to vary the entertainment, ordered him to be bound to a staging of poles, and a fire kindled under him. The first part of the order had been executed; and Ortiz, who was then but eighteen, was stripped and bound to the stake. At that moment, the beautiful daughter of the Cacique, who was about the same age as Ortiz, saw the dreadful fate of the youth; she was moved by compassion; and, throwing herself at her father's feet, begged him to spare the stranger's life. Hirritriqua granted her request; and thus Florida possessed a Pocahontas long before Capt. John Smith owed his life to that renowned maiden.

But Ortiz led a sorry life of it; he was made to labor like a slave, and was subjected to cruel treatment. He would have perished from starvation, had it not been for food furnished him by his lovely protector. One night the Cacique's daughter came to Ortiz, and told him that her father had determined to sacrifice him at the approaching festival; and that all her entreaties had failed to shake his determination. She added that a trusty guide would, that night, lead him to Mucozo, a neighboring chief, who loved her and sought her in marriage; and who, for her sake, would protect him.

At the appointed time, Ortiz met the guide, and was safely conducted to Mucozo, who received him warmly, and finally became greatly attached to him. His hospitable reception displeased Hirritriqua, who made repeated demands on Mucozo to give up the fugitive. The latter, nevertheless, maintained inviolate the sacred rites of hospitality, notwithstanding that the hand of the lovely maiden depended on his acquiescing.

Ortiz had been among the Indians nearly ten years, when De Soto made his appearance; and, as it may well be supposed, he was overjoyed to rejoin his countrymen. His first act was to bring about friendly relations between De Soto and his noble protector, Mucozo. In this he succeeded so well, that whilst the Spaniards remained in that part of the country, they were the best of friends. When, subsequently, the fleet sailed from the neighboring harbor, many things with which the Spaniards did not wish to be encumbered were presented to Mucozo, who found himself abundantly provided for. It took many days for the Indians to carry to their villages, the clothing, weapons, and various stores which the Spaniards had given them.

De Soto, as we have already stated, landed in Florida at Tampa Bay. From that point he took his route to the north and east, passing through Ocala and Tallahassee, from whence he despatched an exploring party, which penetrated far into the interior. Having received a favorable report as to the richness of the country to the north, he pushed forward in that direction, having first sent orders to his fleet to meet him at Pensacola Bay. De Soto crossed the Savannah river, near the present site of the City of Savannah; and entered what is now the State of South Carolina. There a pleasing incident occurred, which we can do no better than relate in the words of Fairbanks, in his " History of Florida:"

"Near the Atlantic coast, in South Carolina, De Soto came into the territories of an Indian Queen, invested with youth, beauty, and loveliness, who is styled by the old Chronicles 'the Ladie of the Countrie.' Upon De Soto's approach, he was met by a lady ambassadress, sister of her Majesty, who delivered a courteous speech of welcome; and, within a little time, the Ladie came out of the town in a chaire, whereon certain of the principal Indians brought her to the river. She entered into a barge, which had the sterne tilted over, and on the floor her mat ready laid, with two cushions upon it, one upon another, where she sat her down, and with her came her principal Indians, in other barges, which did wait upon her.

"She went to the place where the Governor was, and at her coming, she made this speech: 'Excellent lord, I wish this coming of your lordship's into these your countries to be most happy; although my power be not answerable to my will, and my services be not according to my desire, nor such as so high a prince as your lordship deserveth, yet such the good will is rather to be accepted than all the treasures of the world, that without it can be offered; with most unfailable and manifest affection, I offer you my person, lords, and subjects, and this small service.'

"After this courteous and graceful speech from the throne, it may be inferred that so gallant a cavalier as De Soto must have replied in equally complimentary style. The princess caused to be presented to the Adelantado rich presents of the clothes and skins of the country; and, far greater attraction for them, beautiful strings of pearls. Her Majesty, after some maiden coyness, took from her own neck a great cordon of pearls, and cast it about the neck of the Governor, entertaining him with very gracious speeches of love and courtesy; and, as soon as he was lodged in the town, she sent him another present, of not quite so delicate and refined a character, but no doubt considered by her of far greater value, namely, some hens. Perceiving that they valued the pearls, she advised the Governor to send and search certain graves that were in that town, and that they should find many. They searched the graves, and there found ' fourteen measures' of pearls, weighing two hundred and ninety-two pounds, figures of various kinds—little babies, birds, etc., were made of them," reminding one of the recent excavations at Chiriqui.

The people were brown, well made, and well proportioned; and more civil than the other tribes which had been met with in Florida; they were likewise well shod and clothed.

The Spaniards, worried and fatigued by their tedious and fruitless marches, urged their leader to settle in the country, as the climate was mild, the lands rich and productive, and the coast afforded good harbors to shelter their ships. But the Governor replied, that he intended to seek treasures such as Atahualpa, Lord of Peru, possessed. Doubtless the country was a good one, that pearls of value abounded therein, yet there was not sufficient inducement to retain him there. And, as De Soto was firm and decided in his opinion, though giving ear to those of others, his followers acquiesced in his views.

"The fair princess seems to have been ill requited for her hospitable reception of the Spaniards. Held as a hostage (for the good behaviour of the Indians, it is presumed), De Soto insisted upon her accompanying him, which she did for many days; until, one day, turning aside into the forest upon some slight pretext, she disappeared, not without suspicion of design, as there happened to be missing at the same time one of the Spaniards, who, report said, had joined the fair princess for weal or for woe, and had returned with her to her tribe."

From South Carolina, De Soto proceeded

to Georgia, which he penetrated as far as the borders of Tennessee, but failed to find the gold which the natives of the sea-board, with the hope of getting rid of him, had stated would there be found in abundance. Turning his steps to the south-west, he passed through Georgia and Alabama, and reached a point near Mobile, where news was brought that the fleet was awaiting him but a few days' journey off, in the spacious harbor of Ochuse, or Pensacola.

It would have been well if the valorous Spaniard had then abandoned his hopeless enterprise, and had re-embarked his discouraged followers, who had undergone eighteen months of hardship—well, if he had returned to Cuba, where Doña Isabel was anxiously awaiting his coming. But De Soto had decided never to return to his native land until he had discovered the land where wealth abounded. So, binding Ortiz, who, alone besides himself, knew of the proximity of the fleet, to secrecy, he directed his course to the northward and westward; and, after a march fraught with dangers and difficulties, emerged from the swamps and forests of the wilderness, in the Spring of 1541, upon the banks of the Father of Waters, the Mecassabé, near the present site of Memphis.

That year he spent exploring the country west of the Mississippi, and in April he returned to the river, intending to send despatches to the fleet, to be conveyed to Doña Isabel. But the end of the brave soldier was approaching.

In the long marches through the swamps and lowlands, he had contracted a fever, which increased rapidly, and made him aware that his last hour was at hand. He prepared for death with the calmness of a soldier, appointed Louis de Alvarado to the chief command, and required his officers to take the oath to obey and serve him faithfully. This done, the dying Governor called to him his followers, of whom he tenderly took his last leave, calmly addressing them while they wept. De Soto soon after expired.*

Thus perished Hernando de Soto, the most distinguished of the many brave leaders,

* Irving.

whose names are honored as the discoverers and settlers of the Western World. His followers, fearing to bury him on the shore, lest the Indians should desecrate his grave, hollowed out the trunk of a live oak of sufficient diameter to contain the body. Therein they placed the corpse, closed its opening with planking, and at midnight conveyed the remains to mid-stream, where the river was a mile in width and nineteen fathoms deep, They there committed to the deep the mortal remains of their commander.

De la Vega, in his history of the expedition, says: "The discoverer of the Mississippi slept beneath its waters. He had crossed a large part of the Continent in search of gold, and found nothing so remarkable as his burial-place."

Our fair readers will ask what became of the eighteen "measures" of pearls. Alas! in one of the villages where De Soto established his quarters, the natives, at night, fired the building; and it was quite as much as the Spaniards could do to save themselves, much less the pearls which, together with quantities of stores and equipments, were utterly consumed.

De Soto died on 21st May, 1542. His successor, Moscoso de Alvarado, at once summoned a council of his officers to determine the best course to pursue. They decided to leave the country; but how to do so with the least embarrassment was the question. One of the officers, Juan de Anasco, urged the Commander to push through to the frontiers of Mexico, offering to show the way. He insisted that the distance was not great; therefore his advice prevailed, and, in the early part of June, they commenced their march onward.

The Spaniards had not proceeded far on their way, when they discovered that one of their number was missing; a young Cavalier of good family named Diego de Guzman. It appears that the gay Diego, in a foray, had captured a most beautiful Indian girl, with whom he at once fell most desperately in love. As this fair damsel was also missing, the Spaniards concluded the pair had gone off togeth-

456672

er. To make sure that such was the case, the general summoned to him the several chiefs of the province who were in his escort, and gave them to understand that, unless the deserter was brought to his camp, he would be led to believe the Indians had murdered him ; in which case their lives should be the penalty. The alarmed chiefs sent forth their scouts, who soon returned with the news that Guzman was with his fair captive's father, a neighboring Cacique, living on the best in the land and treated with great kindness and distinction. De Gallegos, who was a friend and townsman of De Guzman, wrote beseechingly to him, to remember that he was a Spaniard and a Cavalier, and not to desert his God, his countrymen, and his native land. His eloquent appeal was returned the following day, with the indorsement, in charcoal, " De Guzman."

No other word did the young Cavalier vouchsafe to his companions in arms, but the messenger said he had no intention nor wish to rejoin the army ; whilst the Cacique sent word that his son-in-law, who had restored to him a beloved daughter, was not detained by force, but remained of his own free will. The Governor, upon this, abandoned any further attempt to recover De Guzman, and released the chiefs; who, however, accompanied him to the frontier.*

For many weary months, the brave little army forced its way onward to the westward, reaching the roaming grounds of the Buffalo, and beholding, in the distance, a lofty chain of mountains! At last, despairing of ever reaching Mexico by that route, they reluctantly set out on their return to the Mississippi, which they reached in the Autumn of that year. Wintering in the villages they found upon the banks, and which they fortified, they set to work to build seven vessels for the transfer of the force. Francisco, a Genoese, who had been throughout invaluable to De Soto in building bridges, rafts and boats, superintended the work. He was assisted by several soldiers, who had inhabited the sea-coast of Spain. Notwithstanding their combined efforts, it was not until the early part of

* Irving.

July that the vessels were completed, and the preparations made for taking their departure.

Of the gallant host that had landed with De Soto, but three hundred and fifty survived to embark on the frail vessels comprising the fleet. It started from the mouth of the Arkansas river, upon the bosom of the Father of Waters—the highway, as they hoped, to their distant home.

The Indians had eagerly watched the preparations of the Spaniards; and had sent word far and wide that their common enemies were about to depart, and thus evade the vengeance they had hoped to wreak upon them. The tribes gathered from the surrounding country; they harassed the Spaniards as they passed down the river; and when, at last, they reached the ocean, many had been killed by the arrows of the natives. From the mouth of the Mississippi, the Spaniards coasted along the shores of Louisiana and Texas for nearly two months, and at last reached the Spanish settlements in Mexico. Here they were warmly received by the Viceroy, De Mendozo, who sent those who so desired to Spain, while others he took into his service.

Poor Doña Isabel, the wife of De Soto, during these three years, had never ceased to send fleet after fleet to seek and carry succor to her husband, but they returned without tidings of the Governor. At length, one of her faithful captains reached Vera Cruz, in October, 1543, and there learned the death of De Soto; and that, of his brave men, but three hundred had reached Mexico alive. When this sad news reached Doña Isabel, the blow proved too great for her too bear; and it is said she soon died of a broken heart.

1559—DON TRISTAN DE LUNA.

Not many years elapsed before the Spanish Monarch ordered the Viceroy of Mexico to prepare another expedition for the conquest and settlement of Florida. This expedition, which consisted of fifteen hundred men, set sail, under the command of Don Tristan de Luna, in the Spring of 1559, from the port of Vera Cruz. The fleet reached Pensacola Bay in safety; but a few days after coming to anchor was entirely wrecked, together with the greater part of the supplies. This misfortune, and the unfavorable reports of the country brought to De Luna by scouting parties, which he had sent into the interior, caused the general to render such accounts to the Viceroy as to induce him to recall the expedition—not, however, before its members had suffered privations which equalled those of their predecessors.

De Luna's expedition was the last sent by the Spanish to Florida. At that time the Spaniards regarded as Florida the whole shore of the Continent, from the frontier of Mexico to the Chesapeake. We will conclude this brief history of Florida by narrating only what occurred in the peninsula which now constitutes the State of that name.

1562—THE HUGUENOT SETTLEMENTS.

THE year 1562 marked a new era in the history of Florida and of the Continent. By the withdrawal of De Luna, there was left not a single settlement of Europeans on the Continent of North America beyond the boundaries of Mexico. That year, however, witnessed the first attempt at colonization; and that, too, by the French.

The Huguenots, wearied with struggling against persecution, were seeking homes away from their native land. Encouraged by Admiral Coligny, the head of the Protestant party in France, an expedition for America was fitted out, under Capt. Jean Ribaut, and sailed in February, 1562. Ribaut, with his two vessels, entered the St. John's River on the 1st of May, but remained here a short time only. He proceeded to the northward, until reaching Port Royal harbor, where he determined to found the Huguenot settlement. The site was selected upon an island, a fort erected, in which he left a small garrison, while he returned to France to obtain colonists and supplies for the settlement. On his arrival home, he found the Civil War at its height, which debarred his return to the succor of the colony. The colonists, discouraged by the long absence of their commander, put to sea in a small pinnace which they had constructed, in the mad hope of attempting to reach France. Fortunately they were rescued by an English vessel. Two years later, Coligny being again able to turn his attention to his favorite scheme of colonization, despatched three small vessels to Florida, under command of a companion of Ribaut, named René de Laudonnière.

Laudonnière landed at the present site of St. Augustine; but on the following day entered the St. John's River, where he determined to found a settlement.

The site chosen was at St. John's Bluff, just within the mouth of the River, where the remains of the works they constructed are still said to exist. Laudonnière erected a fort, which he named Fort Caroline, and from it made many excursions to the surrounding country, and seems to have kept on excellent terms with the Indians. He, however, accomplished nothing; and, relying on receiving supplies from France, which of course did not come, the garrison was reduced to the verge of starvation. Their Indian friends got tired of supplying their wants, particularly when they found the stock of "Parisian notions" brought by them was exhausted; they refused longer to bring in provisions. Had it not been for a lovely widow, the Queen of a neighboring tribe, Laudonnière and his companions would have inevitably perished. But the Queen, taking pity of their distress, sent them in the nick of time some boat-loads of corn and beans, which were gladly welcomed by René and his followers. Fairbanks tells us the following:

"In De Bray there is an engraving made from a sketch of Le Moyne's, who accompanied a deputation, representing her Majesty in her state procession. At the head appear two trumpeters blowing upon reeds. Then follow six chiefs bearing a canopied platform, on which is seated, shaded by a leafy canopy, her Majesty, in the person of a beautiful female. Around her neck is a cordon of pearls; bracelets and anklets adorn the person, *et præterea nihil*. On each side walk other chiefs, holding large feather shades or fans; beautiful young girls, bearing baskets of fruits and flowers, follow next to the Queen, and then warriors and her household guards."

In 1565, Coligny, to succor and render permanent the colony in Florida, fitted out seven vessels, upon which he embarked six hundred and fifty persons; comprising not only the representatives of some of the best families of France, but many artisans and their families. The colonists carried with them seed, and implements wherewith to till the land; indeed, every requisite for a permanent settlement. They sailed from Dieppe, under the command of Ribaut, on the 23d of May, 1565; but, encountering stormy weather, it was not till the 29th of August that they reached Fort Caroline, where they found Laudonnière on the eve of departing for France.

In the meantime, whilst Coligny was fitting out this expedition, word had been carried to Spain that the French Huguenots, whom they looked upon as heretics, were on the point of seizing Florida, a land to which the Spaniards claimed exclusive right. Philip II. at once encouraged the fitting out of an expedition to thwart their purpose, and soon found the man whom he needed to accomplish this object.

This was Pedro Menendez, who, having been successful in several naval expeditions, had acquired considerable fame and wealth. His life had been blighted by the loss of a favorite son, who had been shipwrecked on the coast of Florida, on board a treasure ship returning from Mexico.

In the hopes of finding his son, Menendez embarked his fortune in the new expedition, spending a million of ducats for its equipment. The King had been lavish in his promises to assist Menendez, but in the end furnished a single vessel, and two hundred men. In spite of this, Menendez set sail for Florida, from Cadiz, on the 1st of July, 1565, with a fleet of thirty-four vessels. Many of them were ships of from six hundred to a thousand tons, the whole fleet carrying a force of nearly three thousand persons.

It will be noticed that Ribaut's vessels had left France a month in advance of Menendez, but the latter reached the coast of Florida on the same day as the French, though not with the fleet with which he sailed from Cadiz; for only a third of them were with him, the rest having been wrecked or dispersed.

Menendez landed on the coast on the 28th of August, 1565, the fete of St. Augustine, in whose honor he named his settlement—a name it retains at present. From the Indians, Menendez learned that the French were but a few leagues distant to the north, and at the mouth of St. John's river.

The French heard of the arrival of their enemies, and sent out a vessel to reconnoitre. It soon returned, and reported to Ribaut that the Spaniards were engaged in landing at St. Augustine, and in fortifying the place. Ribaut at once resolved to get rid of so dangerous a neighbor by surprising him before he could strengthen his defences. Leaving a small garrison at Fort Caroline, he embarked his whole force; and, on the 10th of September, set sail for St. Augustine. No sooner had he started than a gale arose and drove him far beyond his destination. Menendez, meantime, had started overland to surprise Ribaut. He was guided by two Indian chiefs, enemies of Laudonnière. The country was quasi-impassable, made so by the heavy rains; but Menendez persevered in the march, and at dawn of the third day they arrived at Fort Caroline. Without losing a moment, the Spaniards attacked the fort, which offered but a feeble resistance; it was soon captured. An indiscriminate massacre of men, women and children took place; that, too, to the lasting disgrace of the name of Menendez. Some of his prisoners he hung upon the neighboring trees, placing over them this inscription: " No por Franceses, sino por Luteranos." (" Not as Frenchmen, but as Lutherans.")*

Menendez, having left at Fort Caroline a garrison of three hundred men, returned to St. Augustine, where, this victory over the Huguenots caused great rejoicings. In the midst of the gaieties, word was brought that Ribaut's fleet had been stranded at Matanzas Inlet, some distance below St. Augustine, and that his force was endeavoring to cross to the mainland. Menendez set his army in motion, and soon arrived at the scene of shipwreck.

* Fairbanks.

Here a long parley took place, the French doing their "possible to obtain terms of surrender, by which Menendez would spare their lives and furnish them means to return to their own country." All that could be obtained from him was, "that he would treat them as God directed him." Two hundred of Ribaut's companions, considering the terms extremely suspicious, made their escape in the night, to the southward. In the morning, Ribaut, most of his officers, and one hundred and fifty men, unconditionally surrendered to Menendez, having faith in his clemency. The French claim that Ribaut was promised his life and the lives of his followers, but this the Spanish historians deny. At all events, by the orders of the general, the shipwrecked soldiers were marched into the woods in detached parties and cruelly butchered.

The two hundred who had fled, made their way to Point Canaveral, where they hastily threw up some works to defend them; and then commenced building a vessel from the materials of a wreck which they found there. Upon learning of their whereabouts, Menendez sent them word that if they would surrender, he would protect them and treat them as Spaniards. Most of them accepted his terms, and, singular to narrate, the Spanish commander kept his word. They became a part of the colony, and afterwards some of them returned to France.

The fearful massacres perpetrated by Govnor Menendez created considerable excitement throughout Europe; but Spain approved of the deed, which was commended by Philip II. and his people as a righteous act. France made numerous demands upon the Crown of Spain to revenge the murder of their countrymen; but Charles IX. and his Court felt little sympathy for the misfortunes of the Huguenots, and treated the matter with indifference.

Menendez, having disposed of Ribaut, turned his attention to strengthening the defences of St. Augustine, and placing the settlement on a permanent footing. A strong fort was built, a cathedral and other buildings erected, and magistrates and others appointed to administer the government of the province.

He then set out to explore the shores of the peninsula in search of his long-lost son; and for months persevered in the task. He visited innumerable bays and inlets; and, through his interpreters, sought among the Indian tribes information which might shed light upon the fate of his child. At last, to his great joy, he was told that, near Cape Florida, seven Spaniards, shipwrecked years before, were living with the Indians. Reaching the Indian Settlement, Menendez was bitterly disappointed to find his son was not among them. Sick at heart, he invited the seven Spaniards — who had been with the natives twenty years — on board his vessel, and returned to St, Augustine.

DE GOURGES.

In 1567, Menendez deemed it to his interest to visit Spain, and ordered a vessel to be built to convey him thither. By his command, this craft was of twenty tons burthen. In this little yacht, which would have done credit to herself and her builders in a regatta of the present day, Menendez ran to the Azores in seventeen days, and landed in Spain after the shortest passage of the period. At the Spanish Court he was received with the highest honors; but when he asked for material aid for the struggling colony, and to be reimbursed for the enormous outlay he had made in crushing the Lutheran pirates—as the Huguenots were then termed—he found them slow to respond to his demands. For more than a year he remained in Spain, and at last succeeded "in getting his bill honored," besides being made Governor of Cuba.

He arrived at St. Augustine in the Spring of 1568, and learned with grief and rage that a serious accident had happened to his faithful garrison at Fort Caroline; nothing less than the massacre of the entire party, by De Gourges, the Huguenot.

Dominic de Gourges was a brave soldier; from his early youth he had led a life of adventure; captured by the Spaniards in battle, he had been made a galley-slave. He was also taken by the Turks, but was afterwards recaptured by his countrymen.

Returning from a successful voyage to Brazil, he arrived in France to learn of the massacre of the French at Fort Caroline. From that moment he determined to devote his life and fortune to avenging that dastardly act.

De Gourges did not ask the assistance of the French Government for his proposed expedition; he carefully concealed his designs, but made his preparations with all possible haste. Having secured a permit for a voyage to Africa, to obtain a cargo of slaves, he enlisted about one hundred and eighty soldiers and sailors for the purpose.

After a long and stormy voyage, De Gourges arrived with his three vessels, at Fernandina, then called *La Seine* by the French. It was there that he made his preparations for avenging his countrymen and co-religionists. Among his troops was one who had accompanied the unfortunate Laudonnière, and who understood the language of the natives. This proved a fortunate circumstance; for no sooner had the vessels anchored in the beautiful harbor, than the Indians assembled on the beach to contest the landing of the detested Spaniards, as they supposed De Gourges' party to be. But the above-mentioned soldier explained to the chief, Satourioura, the nature of the expedition. He was pleased with the news, and promised to rally to De Gourges' aid thousands of warriors, who would aid the French in exterminating the common enemy. Then they brought to the French a lad, one Peter De Bré, who had escaped from the massacre at Fort Caroline, and had come to them. He proved of great service as an interpreter and in obtaining correct information as to the strength and position of the Spaniards.[*]

The preparations being completed; accompanied by the forces of his Indian ally, De Gourges set out for Fort Caroline. He reached it, and surprised the garrison, which was unprepared for a land attack.

Finding themselves surrounded, the garrison threw down their arms and attempted to make good their escape. They were, however, either slain or captured. Taking the

[*] Fairbanks.

survivors to the spot where Menendez, three years before, had executed the Huguenots, De Gourges hanged the Spaniards to the branches of the oaks; and, taking down the former inscription placed over the French bodies by the Spaniards, he replaced it with the following; " I do this, not as unto Spaniards, nor as to outcasts, but as to traitors, thieves, and murderers."

De Gourges and his followers then re-embarked, amid a perfect ovation from the Indians, and safely returned to France.

This humiliating blow of De Gourges, together with other discouraging events, damped Menendez's enthusiasm for colonizing. He, nevertheless, made many excursions to the surrounding country, and even reached the shores of the Chesapeake. The Colony, notwithstanding, did not flourish; so, when called to Spain to take command of the Spanish fleet, he was pleased to leave Florida for ever. He died soon after reaching Spain, in 1574, in the fifty-fifth year of his age.

Menendez left the government of Florida in the hands of his relative, the Marquis de Menendez; and, from that time until 1586, its history presents little of interest.

In that year Sir Francis Drake, the English freebooter, on his way to England, surprised and captured St. Augustine, which, at the time, was a well-built and flourishing town. The family of Menendez continued governing Florida for nearly one hundred years. In 1665, an English pirate, Captain John Davis, captured and pillaged the town.

South Carolina, having been settled by the English, constant troubles arose between the Colonists and the Spaniards. Governor Moore, in 1702, attacked St. Augustine, but met with a disastrous repulse. In 1740, Governor Oglethorpe, of Georgia, also met with a like result before the walls of that city. In 1762, Cuba fell into possession of the English; and when peace was declared during the following year, Great Britain transferred it to Spain in exchange for Florida.

Captain James Grant was the first English Governor. One of his earliest acts was the issue of a proclamation referring to the salubrity of the climate, and the extreme age at-

tained by the inhabitants of the country.*
In this, and in other ways, he endeavored to attract emigration to the shores of Florida. In 1766, a certain Dr. Turnbull, a Scotchman, having obtained from the Crown the concession of a large tract of land below St. Augustine, he called it New Smyrna. To it he brought, from Smyrna and the Balearic Isles, fifteen hundred Greeks and Minorcans, whom he settled there.

Ten years later, these colonists secured from the magistrates at St. Augustine, a decree cancelling their agreement with Turnbull; and almost the entire number removed to St. Augustine, and colonized, where their descendants still remain, forming the most industrious and interesting portion of the population.

In 1821, Florida was ceded to the United States. Of the long wars with the Seminole Indians it is unnecessary to remark — the visitor to Florida will continue to find among the old inhabitants many who have gone through those bloody scenes, and

* Fairbanks.

who take interest in narrating them to strangers.

We will here terminate our brief sketch of the history of Florida, referring the reader for more ample information, to the "History of Florida" by Fairbanks; and to Irving's Conquest thereof—of which the writer has availed himself for much of the foregoing information.

FLORIDA;

ITS GEOGRAPHY AND CLIMATE, ETC.

FLORIDA is the most southern of the States of the Union, and extends down to latitude 25° N. The peninsula is four hundred miles in length, with an average width of about one hundred miles. It contains 59,268 square miles of territory, and a population of about two hundred thousand; the white and colored being nearly equal in numbers, the whites slightly predominating.

The surface of the country is remarkably level. The lands in the upper portion of the State, near the boundary of Georgia, are of a rolling character. A large proportion of the land is covered with forests of pine and cypress. The most remarkable feature of the State is its numerous navigable streams and lakes, and its wonderful mineral springs, which probably gave rise to the fable of the Fountain of Rejuvenancy, to which Ponce de Leon aspired possession. The Indians, from the earliest times, had resorted to these fountains for medicinal purposes, and knew well their beneficial effects. Even now the waters continue to enjoy their ancient reputation, and thither strangers repair in search of health.

These springs are the largest in the world —excepting those mentioned by Livingstone as being the source of the Nile. Williams, in his history of Florida, thus describes two of the hundreds which exist in that State.

" The Wakulla River rises about ten miles N. W. from St. Mark's, from one of the finest springs in Florida. It is of an oval form, the largest diameter of which is about six rods. It is of unknown depth and perfectly transparent. In looking into it, the color resembles a clear blue sky, except near the border, where it has a slight tinge of green, from the reflection of the surrounding verdure, which overhangs it in drooping branches and waving festoons. The Eastern side presents a rugged rocky precipice; all else is in an abyss of boundless depth. Squadrons of fish are seen careering round 'their own world' in perfect security.

"The big Spring of Chipola offers a very different scene. Here a river bursts from the earth, with a giant force, from large masses of rugged rocks, with furious rapidity, as though impatient of restraint. The orifice opens to the southwest from a high bank covered with large oak trees. This orifice is thirty feet by eight feet wide. A large rock divides the mouth almost into two parts. This spring at once forms a river six rods wide and eight feet deep, which joins the Chipola River at about ten miles distance."

The River St. John's is one of the most remarkable and beautiful in our country. For a hundred and fifty miles its average width is nearly two miles; and, in many places, it enlarges into lakes ten and twenty miles in width. Of its many beauties we shall have occasion to speak further on.

CLIMATE.

The wonderful salubrity of the climate of Florida is its greatest attraction, and is destined to make it to America what the South of France and Italy are to Europe,—the refuge of those who seek to escape the rigor of a Northern winter. The sudden changes experienced at Nice or Florence are unknown in Florida.

So well convinced are our physicians of this fact, that they now advise their patients to seek health in Florida, within three days' reach of their homes and friends, in lieu of going abroad at a stormy season of the year.

Florida, as a resort for those suffering from pulmonary disease, is preferable to any other portion of America. The census of 1860 furnished the following evidence on this subject. It gives the average number of deaths from Consumption as follows:

    One in 254 in Massachusetts.
    One in 473 in New York.
    One in 757 in Virginia.
    One in 1139 in Minnesota.
    One in 1447 in Florida.

The following Summary of Observations, taken from the "*Army Meteorological Register,*" are introduced to show the equability of the climate of Florida, as compared with that of other parts of the United States:

	Jan.	Feb.	Mar.	Apr.	May.	June
St. Augustine, Fla..	57.03	59.94	63.34	68.78	73.50	79.36
Tampa Bay, " .	61.53	63.54	67.72	71.82	76 64	79.46
Key West, " .	66.68	68.88	72.88	75.38	79.10	81.63
West Point, N. Y..	28.28	28.80	37.63	48.70	59.82	68.41
Fort Snelling, Min.	13.76	17.57	31.41	56.34	58.97	68.46

	July.	Aug.	Sept.	Oct.	Nov.	Dec.	Year
St. Augustine, Fla..	80.90	80.56	78.60	71.88	64.12	57.26	69.61
Tampa Bay, " .	80.72	80.43	78 28	74.02	66.94	61.99	71.92
Key West, "	83.00	82.90	81.92	78.11	74.66	71 03	76.51
West Point, N. Y..	73 75	71.83	64.31	53.04	42.23	31.98	50.73
Fort Snelling, Min.	73.40	70.05	58 86	47.15	31.67	16.8)	46.54

The above indicates the mean temperature, the result of over twenty years' observations.

The sulphur baths at Green Cove Springs, and other points in Florida, have been pronounced as efficacious for the cure of Rheumatism as those of Sharon and Richfield, whilst St. Augustine is the refuge of those afflicted with that dreadful disease, Asthma. We have never heard of an instance where relief was not effected.

HOW TO REACH FLORIDA.

The choice of a route to Florida is, of course, the first and most important considertion to those who intend going thither. According to our opinion, the Steamers of the New York and Charleston, and New York and Savannah lines, offer the best mode of conveyance. They are in all respects the most advisable whether for the invalid or pleasure seeker. The following comprise the vessels running to the places named, and form a splendid fleet of first-class ocean steamers;

NEW YORK AND CHARLESTON LINE.

"Manhattan"—M. S. Woodhull, Commander.
"Champion"—R. W. Lockwood,   "
"Charleston"—James Berry,   "
"James Adger"—T. J. Lockwood, "
"Georgia"— —— Holmes,   "
"South Carolina"—J. T. Beckett, "

Sailing from Pier 29 North River, at 3 P. M., every Tuesday, Thursday, and Saturday. JAS. W. QUINTARD & Co., Agents, corner of Warren and West Streets; or WM. P. CLYDE, 6 Bowling Green.

NEW YORK AND SAVANNAH LINES.

"Leo"—Dearborn, Commander.
"Virgo"—Bulkley,   "

Every Tuesday, from foot of Wall Street, at 3 P. M. MURRAY, FERRIS & Co., Agents, 61 and 62 South Street.

"Herman Livingston"—Cheeseman, Commander.
"General Barnes"—Mallory,   "

Every Thursday, from Pier 43, North River, at 3 P. M. WM. R. GARRISON, Agent, 5 Bowling Green.

"San Jacinto"—Hazard, Commander.
"San Salvador"—Nickerson,   "

Every Saturday, from Pier 43, North River, at 3 P. M. WM. R. Garrison, Agent, 5 Bowling Green.

We refer to advertisements of above companies, which will be found at the end of this volume ; and in the event of any further information being desired, the traveller cannot do better than apply at one of the different offices named, where he will be treated with courtesy, and placed in possession of any information he desires.

The voyage to Charleston or Savannah is a short one, it seldom exceeding sixty hours in time; and experience has proven that the invalid almost invariably improves at sea. The vessels are provided with an excellent table and careful attendance, such comforts as it is impossible to procure on any other route. For those in good health, the trip is a most enjoyable one. The class of passengers availing themselves of these steamers are invariably pleasant and agreeable companions—tourists from all parts of the United States, Boston, New York, Philadelphia, Chicago, St. Louis, Cincinnatti, etc—scarcely a city but is represented on board of them.

Travelers who go by land should leave either by the morning train at 9, or by the 9:30 evening Express, on the New Jersey R. R. The morning train connects at Baltimore with the Steamers of the Bay Line for Norfolk, the least fatiguing route. The capital suppers and comfortable state-rooms furnished on board that line will long dwell in the memory of the Southern traveler. The evening train carries the passenger via Washington and Richmond.

Until recently there was no comfortable resting-place on the road south of Norfolk or Richmond, but now the Purcell House at Wilmington, North Carolina, supplies the want; and, under the care of Colonel Davis, the weary traveler will soon recuperate.

Invalids, and others not pressed for time, should divide the journey thus—Leave New

York by the morning train, and sleep at Washington; pass the following night at Richmond, the third at Wilmington, arriving at Charleston the fourth day. The Arlington at Washington, and Exchange at Richmond, are strictly first-class hotels.

A well-supplied lunch-basket will not be amiss when starting from Richmond to Wilmington, as it is impossible to obtain a good meal on the road.

At Charleston, travelers will find Omnibuses waiting at the Steamship Wharf, and Railway Depot, to convey them to the various Hotels, and to the Steamers of the Florida Line.

CHARLESTON.

Charleston is one of the oldest cities of the Continent (settled in 1679), and is also one of the most interesting and enjoyable. Its situation, almost directly upon the sea, with the waves of the Atlantic in full view from its wharves, is unsurpassed. Its harbor is a fine one, with ample water front to supply the demands of its commerce. Charleston has a beautiful promenade, on the apex of the peninsula on which the city is built, and from it can be viewed Fort Sumter and the islands forming the entrance to the Bay—Morris and Sullivan.

Approaching Charleston by steamer, the city seems to rise from the sea. On misty mornings, the effects of mirage in the harbor are very remarkable. The city then appears raised high above the horizon, and entirely detached from it—whilst Sumter seems thrice its former size. On one or two occasions, during the war, this phenomenon spread consternation through the city, as the whole blockading squadron was made to appear within the obstructions, and fast approaching the wharves. The situation of Charleston for commercial purposes is admirable, being nearer to the ocean than most other Atlantic cities of importance. Its harbor, which is capacious and secure, is easy of access to vessels of large tonnage.

Indeed, Charleston possesses all the requisites of a great commercial seaport, and there is no doubt that, once relieved from her present exorbitant taxation, she will make rapid strides in prosperity. Three great lines of railway connect the city with the interior, by which the products of the South and Southwest can be brought to her wharves at the lowest rates. The recent discoveries of rich deposits of phosphate rock in the districts about the city, have proven to be of great importance, and many millions of dollars and thousands of laborers are profitably employed in digging and preparing it for market.

A very erroneous impression prevails as to the extent of business transacted in Charleston, it being far greater than is generally supposed. Her wholesale trade in dry goods, groceries, etc., is very large—nearly as great as before the war, and greater than any other Southern port, except New Orleans. She receives a large quantity of cotton and lumber, naval stores, rice, and phosphates. In spite of bad government, high taxes, the ravages of fire, and the unfortunate investments in Confederate "securities," Charleston is undoubtedly progressing, and but few years will be required to restore her to her former position.

A growing confidence in the final restoration of an honest State government is again attracting capital from abroad; and many transactions have of late taken place in real estate, within the city, on terms which, to those accustomed to the prices current in Northern cities, would seem preposterously low. Fine dwellings, with beautiful gardens attached thereto, are selling for from six to ten thousand dollars—in many instances the same buildings having originally cost double that sum.

The resources of Charleston for a pleasant sojourn are varied, and visitors, in great numbers, avail themselves of them during the winter months. The hotels have always been celebrated for their comfort and good cheer. Unfortunately one of the favorite resorts, the "Mills' House," is now closed; but the "Charleston," a strictly first-class hotel, is kept in excellent style, and has been recently enlarged to meet the demand of increased business. It is admirably managed and ap-

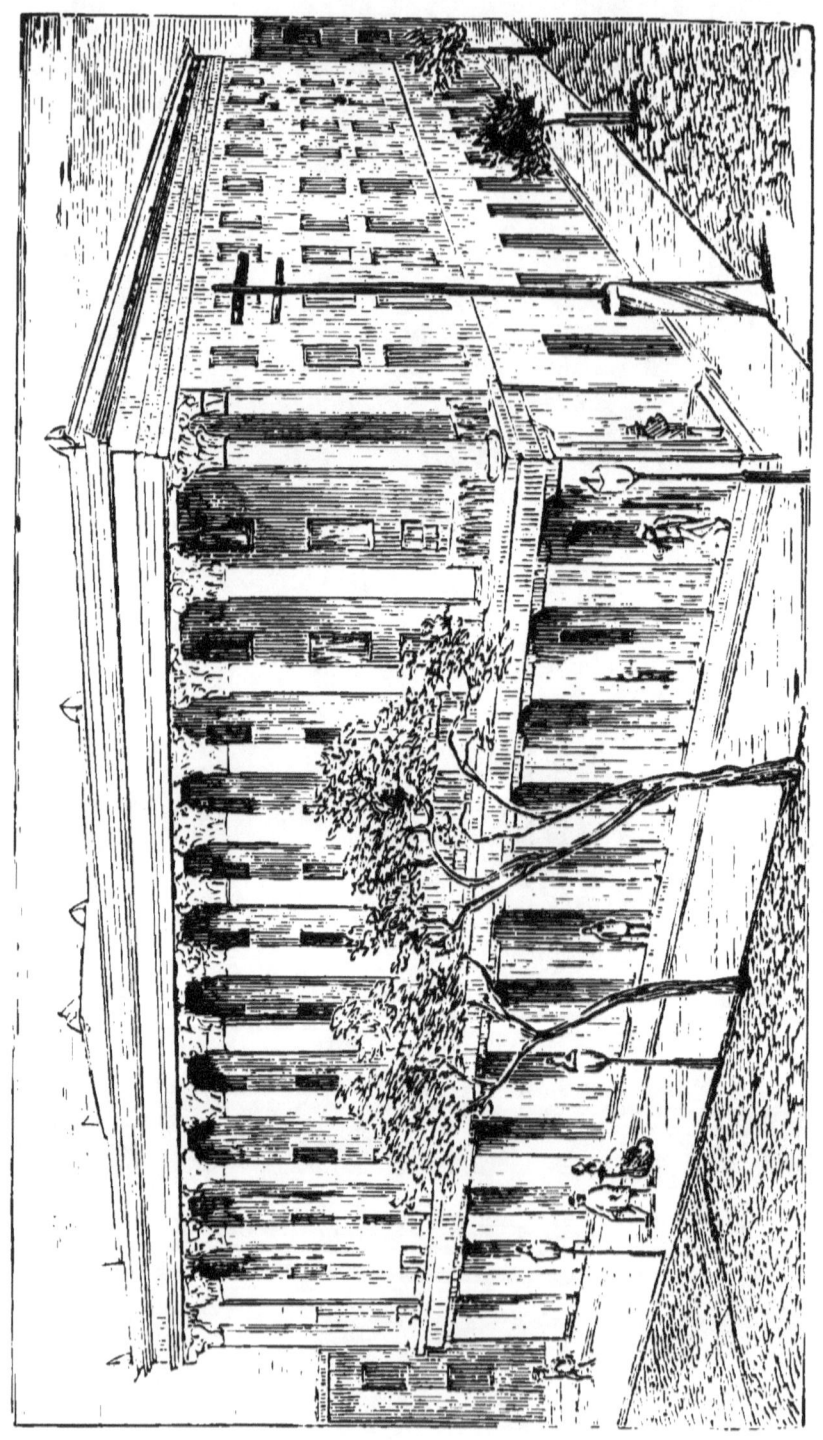

THE "CHARLESTON" HOTEL, CHARLESTON, S. C.

(To face p. 73.)

pointed, and the building is one of the ornaments of the city.

The Artesian Baths attached to the house form one of its greatest attractions. The waters, which flow direct from the wells, are equal in softness to the most famous springs of Germany.

In the building is an office where tickets to Florida can be obtained. At the office of the hotel carriages can be procured to visit several places of interest in and about the city.

The "Pavilion Hotel" is a well-kept, comfortable house, to whose advertisement we call attention.

OBJECTS OF INTEREST.

The public institutions of Charleston are numerous, and well worthy of a visit. The Orphan Asylum is an exceedingly fine building, from whose cupola a most extensive view of the city and harbor can be obtained. St. Nicholas' and St. Philip's Churches are fine edifices—the former was built from designs of Sir Christopher Wren, who was also the architect of the building known as the Old Post-office.

This building is one in which many prominent historical incidents were enacted. It was the Government House in the Colonial days; and during the Revolution its cellars were the dungeon in which the British confined the prominent patriots—from it Hayne was led to execution. Charlestonians regard the building with interest and affection, and hailed with pleasure the act of the Washington government in repairing it, for it had fallen into almost total ruin. A great number of shells, during the bombardment, had traversed it from roof to cellar. It is again used as the Post-office, and, though much altered, still bears traces of its original architecture.

The church-yards of Charleston contain many ancient and interesting monuments, some bearing exceedingly quaint inscriptions. Calhoun's tomb is in St. Philip's yard.

The Battery, lined with rows of beautiful residences, is the favorite afternoon promenade. At sunset, the visitor, leaning over the parapet rail, watching the waves break against the sea-wall, cannot but appreciate the beauty of the scene. Seaward lies Sumter, with a fleet of vessels, large and small, passing to and fro around the fortress. On the right is James' Island, with the grove of giant pine trees, known as the Hundred Pines, standing out in bold relief against the sky; whilst, looking up the Ashley, a view is obtained of a beautiful river, with banks lined with groves of magnolia and live oaks.

King Street is the Broadway of Charleston, where the traveller can supply himself from stores well filled with every commodity.

The markets form a point of interest, and should be visited. On Saturday night the scene presented is curious, and peculiarly Charlestonian.

There are several beautiful drives in the environs of Charleston; to Magnolia Cemetery,—to Lowndes' Avenue, to Belvidere,—to the Four Mile House, and to the Ship-yard. The roads, in most places, are bordered by live oaks, magnolias, and pines, from whose branches hang masses of gray moss, presenting a most unique appearance—whilst, in the Spring, the hedges are filled with wild flowers—the beautiful Cherokee rose and yellow jessamine growing in tropical profusion, and climbing high among the branches of the trees.

The Charleston phosphates afford interest to the agriculturist and the naturalist, who should not fail to visit the region of their whereabouts. A recent work says:

"In this region are found the most wonderful remains of ancient and extinct species of animals. There are whole acres richly studded with fossils. Among these have been recognized the bones of the Mammoth, Mastodon, Megatherium, Mylodon, Megalonyx, Phocodon, and several varieties of the Sauri; also teeth and bones of the shark, and numerous other fishes in great variety; also teeth and bones of the horse, dog, sheep, ox and hog, differing but little, if at all, from those belonging to our present domestic animals. Pieces of pottery have been discovered combined with stone hatchets, etc., in the same bed, and almost identical in their character with remains of the extinct animals, etc., found some years since, near Abbeville, in France. It is said that human bones were found, but the evidence to that effect is not positive. This strange collection, this sepulchre of the ages, where animals, now extinct, sleep side by side with others; the ancestors, perhaps, of our daily companions—where men, beasts, reptiles and fishes, would seem to have found a common grave—these fossils occur in the post-pleiocene strata. They have been described in the scientific journals by Professor Holmes, whose articles attracted many savans; among them, Agassiz, Count Portalis and Leidy."

A visit to the Phosphate works in the vicinity of the city, will well repay one. The rock can be procured in Charleston, without the labor of a journey to the diggings. The trade in fertilizers has assumed extensive proportions. Since its discovery, its production has reached a figure representing several millions of dollars annually.

No one should leave Charleston without

visiting the numerous points of interest in the harbor, made memorable by the stubborn conflicts between the Confederates and the forces of the Federal Army and Navy. The excursion to Forts Sumter and Moultrie, and to the batteries on Morris, Sullivan and James' Islands, is a delightful one, and can be safely made in the comfortable yacht Eleanor, which makes several trips daily from the Florida Steamship Wharf.

SAVANNAH.

The visitor will find Savannah a beautiful city, abounding in pleasant walks and drives. It is one of the most prosperous cities of the South; one which does an enormous business in merchandize, cotton and lumber. Its wharves, during most of the year, are crowdded with vessels.

The situation of Savannah, her perfect railroad facilities, etc., guarantees her a brilliant future. She already receives nearly one sixth of the cotton crop, and new avenues to trade are constantly increasing. Much of the pros-

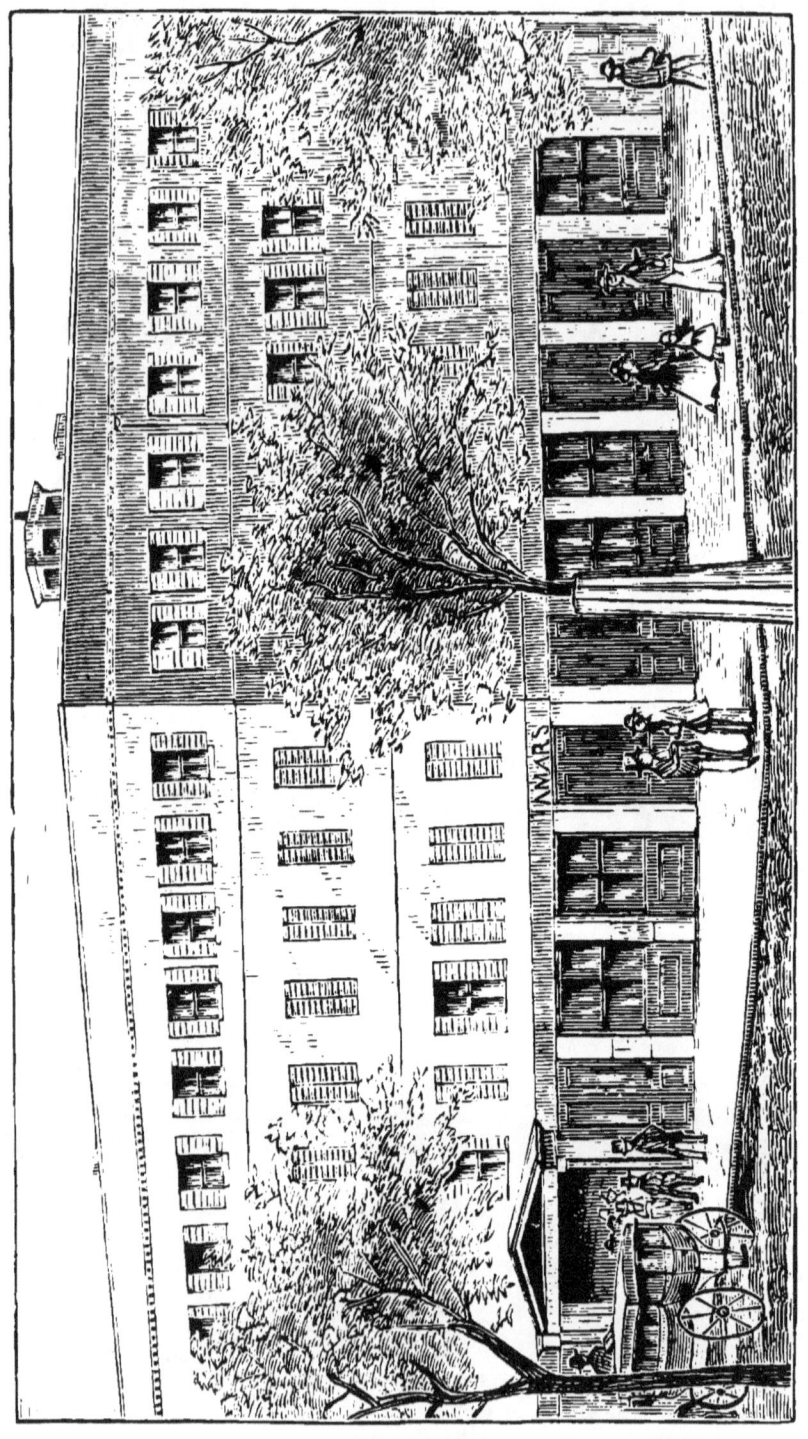

THE "PULASKI" HOTEL, SAVANNAH.

(To face p. 79.)

perity of the city can be directly traced to the liberal course pursued by the manager of her great railroad, "The Georgia Central." This road, with its branches and connections, keeps up constant communication with Augusta, Macon, Atlanta, Columbus, Montgomery, and New Orleans, etc.; it is pronounced to be the best-managed road in the Southern country.

Savannah possesses several excellent hotels —the Pulaski, long considered one of the best at the South, has recently been put in complete order—refurnished, and many improvements made in its interior. On the opposite side of Johnson Square, will be found the Screven House, which shares with the Pulaski a well-deserved popularity. It is admirably kept.

The Pavilion,—beautifully situated on Bull Street, is now in the hands of Mr. Fernandez, whom visitors to the Pulaski in former years will no doubt remember. It is spoken of as excellently kept; and its charges, as will be seen from the advertisement, are moderate.

Savannah derives its principal beauty from its wide streets flanked with magnificent trees. The oak, the magnolia, and the Pride of India, shade the way to pedestrians, making walking agreeable. Forsyth Park is undoubtedly one of the prettiest spots in America; it is a favorite resort of the *beau-monde* of the city. At early evening the visitor will see the loveliest faces; such beauties as will compare favorably with those of Baltimore.

Several pleasant excursions can be made from Savannah; one to Bonaventure, a beautiful cemetery, shaded by the most remarkable grove of live-oaks in the world. Those splendid trees flank the avenues; their branches interlacing high overhead, thus forming arches whose symmetry is admirable. From every branch hang festoons of Spanish moss, looking as though the whole grove were draped in mourning in respect to the dead who repose within their everlasting shadow. The place is beautiful beyond description; it impresses the visitor with gloomy thoughts; one feels relieved when, emerging therefrom, he visits Thunderbolt, where on

FORSYTH PARK, SAVANNAH. (To face p. 80.)

the pleasant bank of the Vernon river his gloom is soon overcome. The oysters found there are excellent, and a lunch or dinner can at all times be obtained. The ladies need not be afraid of the milk-punches; they form a specialty of the place, and their fair sisters of Savannah consider them "quite the thing."

White Bluff, ten miles from the city, is reached by an excellent well-shaded road; a day can be agreeably spent there. Fish dinners are the speciality at Mrs. Sylvester's; they are such as Greenwich never gave to Londoners.

From Charleston and Savannah, the fine New York built Steamers "Dictator" and "City Point" furnish a tri-weekly line to Florida. We do not hesitate to pronounce the route the cheapest, safest and only comfortable way of reaching the different resorts in that State. By any other route, many changes of conveyance are made imperative; causing great inconvenience and suffering to the invalid traveller. By embarking on the "Dictator" or "City Point" this is avoided, and the visitor is landed, without change of conveyance at the very doors of the principal hotels of Florida. The steamers proceed directly to:—

 Fernandina,
 Jacksonville,
 Magnolia,
 Green Cove Springs,
 Picolata,
 Tocoi,
 Palatka,

Connecting with cars at Tocoi for—

 St. Augustine,

And at Palatka with comfortable steamers for—

 Enterprise,
 Mellonville,
 Sanford,

and the Indian River Country, as well as with boats for the Oclawaha River

These steamers are prepared expressly for the Florida route, and are unsurpassed for speed, safety, and comfort. They are under the command of experienced officers, Captains Vogel and Fitzgerald, who have spent most of their life on this route, never meeting with an accident during the many years of their service thereon.

A large sum was spent, last summer, in refitting these vessels with new boilers, and in supplying them with the latest improvements for comfort and convenience. The staterooms are clean and comfortable, whilst the table is provided with every luxury that Charleston, Savannah, and Florida markets can produce.

Leaving Charleston in the evening, the steamers arrive at Savannah early in the morning, and leave soon after for Fernandina. Possessing great speed, they rapidly run along the Sea Islands of Georgia; and, as westerly winds prevail during the winter, the traveler is—from the smoothness of the sea, and the balmy temperature of the air—reminded of the Mediterranean. The effect is beneficial to the invalid, whose strength is renewed, and appetite increased by the change; so much so, as to do justice to the excellent meals supplied by the steamers. New York supplies them with beef, mutton, and poultry; whilst Florida,

Georgia, and South Carolina, are put under contribution for fish and game.

We have known several persons who, for months before leaving home, were unable to eat a good repast, heartily enjoy their meals during the entire trip from Charleston to Florida, arriving at their destination much improved, and in striking contrast to others who were half the winter in recovering from the fatigues of reaching the St. John's river by land.

A uniform temperature is kept up in the saloons and state-rooms of the vessels, which are heated by steam. This will be appreciated by those who have experienced the varied temperature in railway cars, heated by a stove.

The decks of the "Dictator," and "City Point," in the traveling season, present an animated appearance, as the vessel glides along the coast of Georgia. The passengers group about, conversing on the subject of their voyage; listening to the experience of those who are familiar with the localities to be visited; or whiling away the hours playing cards or chess, etc. Boston, New York, and Philadelphia, are often found represented in the same party; and under the pleasant influences of the southern air, good fellowship prevails. The invalids, who find themselves in better health and spirits, propose hunting and fishing parties to the Indian River, and elsewhere. Indeed, the very nature of the conversation, and the hopeful looks of the sufferers, tell, already, the effects of the climate.

FERNANDINA.

In the evening, the steamer reaches Fernandina, which is beautifully situated on Amelia Island. It possesses an excellent harbor, easy of access to vessels of large tonnage; it has a considerable and increasing trade in cotton and lumber. It is the terminus of the railroad to Cedar Keys, where a line of steamers connects it with Havana and New Orleans.

The Ridell House and Norwood House are well-kept establishments.

From Fernandina, the traveler can reach

Quincy, Tallahassee, Live Oak and other points on the interior, by the "Jacksonville, Pensacola, and Mobile Railroad."

ST. JOHN'S RIVER.

A FEW hours after leaving Fernandina, the steamer enters the beautiful St. John's. Near the entrance is to be seen the St. John's Bluff, the site of Fort Caroline, and of the scenes rendered memorable by the massacres of Spaniard and Huguenot. The officers of the steamers are well versed in the history of the country, and are willing to impart much interesting information to the traveler. They will always be found ready to promote the welfare of the travelers, and to make the trip a comfortable and pleasant one. Ladies and children are especially cared for by an attentive stewardess, whose duty it is to see that their wants are supplied.

The trip up the St. John's is unlike any other—the river presenting scenes entirely novel. The stream is in most places two miles in width, and often spreads out into great lakes from twelve to twenty miles wide. The St. John's is undoubtedly the most beautiful of southern rivers, and was well named by the Indians " the String of Pearls." The steamer makes the trip from the mouth of the river to Palatka in about six hours, stopping at all the principal landings, which we shall now describe.

JACKSONVILLE.

This is the most important town in Florida, and is the great entrepot of the trade of the middle and eastern sections of the State. Its communication with the interior is perfect, not only by the St. John's River, but also by an extended line of railway, connecting it with Tallahassee and other important places. Were this road and its branches managed in the interest of Jacksonville, a very large cotton trade would centre here ; but, at present, the strange spectacle is presented of an important sea-port, the natural outlet of the product of an enormous extent of the finest cotton-fields in the South, doing comparatively nothing in the great staple. We learn an effort is being made by the merchants of Jacksonville, which cannot but receive the support of every one interested in the future of the city and state, to bring back to its natural channel a business which would create a degree of prosperity little dreamed of. As it is, Jacksonville can boast the most progressive business community of any town of its size in the South, and the rapid strides it has made within the past few years, would do credit to any city of the North or West.

Jacksonville is the centre of the great lumber trade of Florida; it employs an immense number of vessels carrying cargoes of Southern pine to all parts of the world. These, and the innumerable steamers plying on the St. John's, gives the river a most animated and agreeable appearance.

During the past two years, the number of visitors to Jacksonville has doubled; but, fortunately the hotel accommodations have kept pace with the demand.

The Grand National is an excellent Hotel recently completed and admirably situated, commanding an extended view of the river. Its proprietor, Mr. McGinley is a celebrated host at the South.

The "St. James" is a fine building, of imposing appearance, capable of accommodating about three hundred guests. It contains many large, well furnished, and comfortable apartments, and is very highly spoken of. Its present proprietor is Mr. J. B. Campbell, of Massachusetts, which fact alone will carry to it many guests.

The "Metropolitan," situated close to the landing place of the Florida steamers, is also a new hotel, well appointed and admirably kept.

There are also numerous boarding houses, said to be exceedingly good, and where the prices are reasonable. The best are said to be, Mrs. Hudnall's, St. John's House; Mrs. Buffington's; Mrs. Atkins', and Mrs. Day's; whilst the "Sisters of St. Joseph" have a house apart from their Academy, where a moderate number can be accommodated and made very comfortable.

The traveler will be able to spend the time very agreeably at Jacksonville. There is a daily communication with the North, and letters and newspapers are regularly received. The telegraph is also in operation, affording, at all times, the means of immediate intelligence. At the "Ambler Bank" one can negotiate his business, whilst Adams' Express is at hand to take charge of the parcels. Boating, sailing, and drives to the pleasant suburbs of the town, will help to wile away the days.

Before leaving for the interior, it would be well to provide such little supplies as old travelers are wont to make. The gentlemen will find at Bettelini and Togni's an excellent supply of wines and delicacies. This is explained, when we say they have one or two vessels trading between Jacksonville and France, bringing them an unadulterated supply of various kinds. The ladies will find at Furchgott, Benedict & Co.'s a good selection of dry goods, etc.; and at Greenleaf's, a stock of Florida curiosities, from which selections of souvenirs of their trip can be obtained, such as alligator teeth, St. Augustine sea-beans, curlew wings, plumes for hats, etc., etc.

ST. JOHN'S RIVER.

The trip up the river is one of the most

delightful possible. By the way, it should not be forgotten that "up the river," is down the river, as the St. John's rises in the Everglades south, and flows almost due north; the reverse of the course pursued by most rivers in the world.

The shores of the St. John's are wanting in what forms the great beauty of the Hudson—the hills and mountains, to enhance the grandeur of the landscape. Here the banks seldom rise more than twenty feet above its placid waters. The scene is, however, most picturesque; and, as the steamer glides over the mirror-like surface, the passengers are loud in their expressions of admiration. From time to time groves of orange trees, covered with golden fruit, are passed — the contrast between them and the forests of oak, pine, and cypress, which fringe the shores, making an agreeable variety.

MANDARIN.

Mandarin, the first landing-place of any importance, is a small village on the east bank, nearly an hour's sail from Jacksonville. It is one of the earliest settlements, but suffered much during the Indian troubles. It possesses several fine orange groves, one of the finest of which belongs to Mrs. Harriet Beecher Stowe, who spends her winters here. Several Indian mounds are to be found in the neighborhood.

HIBERNIA.

Hibernia, about 8 miles further on, is one of the most pleasant resorts. Mrs. Fleming has here an excellent house. The country about abounds in beautiful groves of oak, etc.

MAGNOLIA.

Magnolia, 27 miles from Jacksonville, on the west bank, is a prepossessing place, which possesses an excellent and well-patronized hotel, once much resorted to by Northern visitors.

GREEN COVE SPRINGS.

On rounding Magnolia Point, the steamer

enters a beautiful bay where, in full view, lies GREEN COVE SPRINGS, the Saratoga of the St. John's. It is already a favorite resort, which possesses several of the best hotels in Florida. Its importance is assured; and several wealthy families have expressed the intention of building winter residences in its neighborhood.

The "Clarendon House" is admirably kept by Harris, Applegate & Co. It has attached to it the celebrated Warm Sulphur Spring— the great attraction to the place. The spring discharges 3,000 gallons of water per minute, at a temperature of 78°. This water is said to be as valuable for its medicinal properties as that of Sharon or Richfield, and is reported to have effected many remarkable cures. The "Union House" is also a first-class hotel, extensively patronized by New Yorkers and Bostonians.

PICOLATA.

Picolata is the site of a Spanish settlement, made shortly after the founding of St. Agustine. It consists of but one house.

TOCOI.

Tocoi is the terminus of the St. Augustine Railroad; it is here that passangers for that city disembark. The road in question, we learn, has been put in good order, and the managers promise a quick and comfortable transit to the ancient city.

ORANGE MILLS.

is about 65 miles from Jacksonville, and is prettily located on the east bank. Mr. Cole's residence here is surrounded by orange groves.

PALATKA.

Palatka, the terminus of the route of the "Dictator" and "City Point," is a flourishing town of about fifteen hundred inhabitants. It is situated on the west bank of the St. John's, 75 miles from Jacksonville. Passengers, bound beyond, are transferred to the steamer "Starlight" and other boats bound for Enterprise,

Mellonville, Indian River, etc., as well as for all other points on the Ocklawaha. Palatka is highly recommended by physicians as a resort for invalids.

Palatka possesses two excellent hotels—the "St. John's" and the "Putnam House." A recent writer in *Harper's* thus describes his experience at the former. Arriving at Palatka he found the "Starlight" so crowded that no state-room was to be had.

"This apparent misfortune proved our greatest happiness; for, lying over at Palatka, at the St. John's Hotel, we obtained delicious food wherewith to assuage the pangs of hunger. Think not, good reader, this is an unnecessary exhibition of feeling over a small matter; for great had been our suffering, and great was our delight. Delicious waffles, noble wild turkey (nobly served), tender lamb, adolescent chicken, light, sweet bread, potatoes, green pease, and other delicacies that ravished the heart and made glad the digestive apparatus."

The same writer describes the trip on the "Starlight" to Enterprise thus:

"As the steamer plowed along its narrow channels, the water rushing in to fill the vacuum she made, would sway the countless lily-pads and bending ferns to and fro, sometimes baptizing them with its generous flood. The forest trees were the same all along the way. Cypress, maple, pine, and live-oak, while the palmetto would sometimes choke out the other growths, and send forth, for acres around, its umbrella-shaped tops. The vines grew everywhere, and along the banks would trail in masses, sweeping the dark waters with their leafy fringe. Often the dead, gaunt form of some towering pine would rise above its fellows; and here the osprey would leave his nest, secure from harm; and then, sitting upon some outstretched limb, would dash from his height into the waters and bear his prey aloft to his waiting offspring.

"Now and then the steamer would shoot into a more open space, and where there did not appear to be any outlet—where the bow of the boat seemed about to be crushed against the land; but it parted before us, and what appeared to have been the solid earth was but a floating island, which went dancing and torn in the wake behind us, its long roots thrown up to the troubled surface of the water. At every turn in the river—and it had an endless twist and turn—the tall forms of the blue-and-white heron would rise from the shallow waters and fly before us.

"Thousands of ducks were feeding among the water plants; and not seldom it was a comical sight when, coming suddenly upon them, they would attempt to rise; but, too fat to achieve speedy flight, would tremble and flutter, and finally scamper away into the tall weeds. Later in the day, the sun came out, and then the torpid bodies of huge alligators would be seen lying on the banks. To me the most charming feature of the trip to Enterprise was the presence of the large birds I saw for the first time. Nothing could be more beautiful than the flocks of white swan, curlew, cygnets, and heron constantly rising before us."

ENTERPRISE.

Enterprise possesses a large well-kept hotel, the BROCK HOUSE, the head-quarters of the sportsmen who rendezvous here to perfect their arrangements for excursions into the surrounding country. Small steamers sail-boats, etc., can be chartered there at moderate rates, with experienced persons to guide the stranger through the hunting-grounds, or to the best fisheries on Indian River.

No part of the United States, nor of North America, affords finer sport than Florida. Game of all kinds abounds.

It is during the cold season, when the northern sportsmen are confined indoors, that the game is most plentiful in Florida. Deer, bear, wild cat, raccoon, 'possum, wild turkey, ducks, geese, snipe, woodcock, quails, partridge, and curlews, are plentiful, and offer fine hunting; while the rivers, bays, and lakes, invite the stranger to the pleasures of the rod, filled as they are with schools of the finest fish.

Enterprise is 200 miles south of Jacksonville. Its climate is, consequently, much milder—frost being almost unknown.

In the vicinity are some fine orange groves, whilst a remarkable sulphur spring, of great extent, and nearly a hundred feet in depth, is the curiosity of the place.

On the opposite shore of Lake Munroe is

MELLONVILLE.

Mellonville affords good accommodation to the visitor. It possesses several hotels and boarding-houses. Its orange groves are among the largest and most productive in Florida.

SANFORD.

Extending from Mellonville, five miles along Lake Munroe, and down the St. John's, is "Sanford's Grant." It is owned by Henry S. Sanford, our former Minister to Belgium. He has located here the town of Sanford, which commands the traffic of the river, and the rich agricultural country back of it. It is destined to be the most important place in the Upper St. John's. Mr. Sanford has laid out roads, built mills, and brought over near one hundred Swedes, who have formed a flourishing colony, where they have secured permanent labor, and demonstrated the healthfulness of the climate. Mr. Sanford has large plantations of bananas; one of which, St. Gertrude, is of 100 acres, the largest on the Continent. His idea is to prove that capital, applied to the production of semitropical fruits in Florida, will not only be remunerative, but that Florida can make us independent of the world for those products.

At Sanford is located the Mellonville Post-office. There is a fine Episcopal Church, with the only spire to be seen between Key West and St. Augustine. Its parsonage is nearly completed. It is being erected by Mrs. Sanford, who is helped by friendly contributions. A large school-house is to be erected there; and a first-class hotel, in contemplation, will be located near the Warm Sulphur Springs of St Gertrude.

One of these springs, which made its appearance in January, 1872, is said to be of greater volume than that at Green Cove Springs. The salubriousness and mildness of the climate of Sanford, the beauty of the country, its miles of lovely drives through the pine openings, interspersed with beautiful lakes, with unbounded resources for the sportsman, etc., points this out as destined to be a favorite place of resort for the Northerner who seeks health, combined with relaxation, from business.

As for the orange, the experience of the

past few years has demonstrated that the south side of Lake Munroe is the best portion, on the St. John's, for its culture, as it is protected from the north wind by that large body of tepid water beyond the reach of injurious frosts.

Back of Sanford are several groves much frequented by visitors, and said to produce $2,000 worth of oranges per acre. Many new groves are being laid out, in and about the place.

ST. AUGUSTINE.

We must now return to Tocoi, and take the cars for St. Augustine. On a fine day, the three hours' ride through the pines is a pleasant one.

St. Augustine, historically, is the most interesting city in Florida, while its quaint appearance makes it different from any other city in the land. It was an important town half a century before the landing of the pilgrims. In the preceding chapters, the reader will find recorded most of the important events which mark its history.

FORTIFICATION IN ST. AUGUSTINE. (To face p. 102.)

The ST. AUGUSTINE HOTEL and the MAG-
NOLIA HOUSE are the principal ones; they
are excellently kept. Numerous boarding-
houses also afford good accommodation, at
moderate prices.

St. Augustine is the *point-de-mire* of Florida.
To visit the State, without seeing its quaint
old city, would be like traveling through Italy
without entering the gates of Rome.

St. Augustine is unlike any other city of
this continent; yet, it must be acknowledged
that, the innovations are gradually effacing its
Spanish or Moresque peculiarities. Already
the customs are Americanized; the Spanish
cavalier is of the past, so is the duena, and
the senorita, whom she so carefully guarded.

But there are monuments of its founders
which have withstood time, and whose soli-
dity of construction has not been affected by
the elements—monuments which tell of past
glories, and of the high state of the military
art of engineering, at the date of the settlement of St. Augustine.

Rev. H. Clay Trumbull describes the city
as follows:

"Its principal building material is a unique conglomerate of fine shells and sand, known as coquina rock, found in large quantities on Anastasia Island, at the entrance of the harbor, and which is easily cut in blocks to be laid in courses, and perhaps covered over with stucco. The streets are quite narrow: one, which is nearly a mile long, being but fifteen feet wide, and that on which a principal hotel stands being but twelve feet, while the widest of all is but twenty-five feet. An advantage of these narrow streets in this warm climate is, that they give shade, and increase the draft of air through them as through a flue. Indeed, some of the streets seem almost like a flue, rather than an open way; for many of the houses, with high roof and dormer windows, have hanging balconies along their second story, which seem almost to touch each other over the narrow street; and the families sitting in these of a warm evening, can chat confidentially, or even shake hands with their over-the-way neighbors.

"The street walls of the houses are frequently extended in front of the side garden—the

"OLD ENTRANCE GATE," ST. AUGUSTINE. (To face p. 105.)

house roof, and perhaps a side balcony, covering this extension; or the houses are built around uncovered courts, so that, passing through the main door of a building, you find yourself still in the open air, instead of within the dwelling. These high and solid garden walls are quite common along the principal streets; and an occasional latticed door gives you a peep into the attractive area beyond the massive structure, with perhaps a show of huge stone arches, or of a winding staircase between heavy stone columns, or of a profusion of tropical vegetation in the winter garden, bringing to mind the stories in poem and romance of the loves of Spanish damsels, and of stolen interviews at the garden gate, or elopements by means of the false key or the bribed porter. The principal streets were formerly well paved or floored with shell concrete, portions of which are still to be seen above the shifting sand; and this flooring was so carefully swept, that the dark-eyed maidens of old Castile, who then led in society here, could pass and repass without soiling their satin slippers. No rumbling wheels were permitted to crush the firm road-bed, or to whirl the dust into the airy verandas, where, in undisturbed repose, sat the indolent Spanish dons and dames.

"Built as a military town, the city was formerly walled across its northern end; which sufficiently protected it, as it stands on a peninsula nearly surrounded by the St. Sebastian River and St. Augustine Bay. The gateway of the old wall still stands, and is quite an imposing ruin, with ornamented lofty towers and loopholed sentry-boxes. The ditch before the old wall (or possibly it was a stockade, except at the gateways) is clearly marked, and even yet partially filled at high tides. It runs from shore to shore, and was evidently broad and deep. The old fort, once called San Juan, then St. Marco, but now known as Fort Marion, is a curiosity. It stands on the seafront, at the upper end of the town, the wall or stockade formerly running from it to the gateway, and west to the river. Its material is the inevitable coquina rock. It was a hundred years in building. While owned by the British, it was said to be the "prettiest fort in the king's dominion." Its castellated battlements; its formidable bastions, with their frowning guns; its lofty and imposing sally-port, surrounded by the royal Spanish arms; its portcullis, moat, drawbridge; its circular and ornate sentry-boxes at each principal parapet-angle; its commanding look-out tower; and its stained and moss-grown massive walls —impress the external observer as a relic of the distant past; while a ramble through its heavy casemates; its crumbling Romish chapel, with elaborate portico and inner altar, and holy-water niches; its dark passages, gloomy vaults, and more recently discovered dungeons—brings you to ready credence of its many traditions of inquisitorial tortures, of decaying skeletons found in the latest-opened chambers, chained to the rusty ringbolts, and of alleged subterranean passages to the neighboring convent.

"These stories lose none of their force by being recited in the fitful light of the dim lamp of your military guide, as you follow him into the damp and noisome recesses to the echo of your own foot-fall, or the grating lock and creaking hinge of the slow-swinging ancient doors. Many a dark tally-list on the moldering walls, or a rudely-executed sketch, shows how the dragging days were noted or employed by weary prisoners of long ago; and the narrow loopholes are shown through which the two Seminole chiefs attempted their escape, one making it good, and the other sticking fast in the crevice until he was rescued with barely his life remaining. At the time of Gen. Oglethorpe's attack on·St. Augustine, the old fort, or castle as it was then called, stood a bombardment of thirty-eight days from batteries erected on Anastasia Island. But the injury to the fort was only slight; for the spongy walls of coquina received and imbedded the heavy shot, as would the embankment of a modern earthwork. The marks left by the shot are plainly seen to-day. But time is at length doing its work with the old fort. Its walls are showing huge fissures, and on recent inspection it was declared unfit for further defensive service.

" In the buildings of the town are some remains of elegance, as well as much of antiquity.

STREET SCENE IN ST. AUGUSTINE.   (To face p. 109.)

The cathedral is unique, with its belfry, in the form of a section of a bell-shaped pyramid, its chime of four bells in separate niches, and its clock, together forming a cross. The oldest of these bells is marked 1682. The old convent of St. Mary's is a suggestive relic of the days of papal rule. The new convent is a tasteful building of the ancient coquina. The United States' barracks, recently remodeled and improved, are said to have been built as a convent or monastery. The old government house, or palace, is now in use as the post-office and United States' court-rooms. At its rear is a well-preserved relic of what seems to have been a fortification to protect the town from an over-the-river or inland attack. An older house than this, formerly occupied by the attorney-general, was pulled down a few years ago. Its ruins are still a curiosity, and are called (though incorrectly) the governor's house.

"The 'Plaza de la Constitution' is a fine public square in the centre of the town, on which stand the ancient markets, and which is faced by the cathedral, the old palace, the convent, a modern Episcopal church, and other fine structures. In the centre of the plaza stands a monument, erected in honor of the Spanish Liberal Constitution. When the Constitution was abolished, these monuments in all dominions of the crown were to be destroyed; but a compromise was effected on this by the removal of the inscribed tablets. On the cession of Florida to the United States, the long-concealed tablets were brought from their hiding-places, and re-inserted in the monument. On this plaza were burned effigies of John Hancock and Samuel Adams, early in our Revolution, while the British held Florida.

"The old Huguenot burying-ground is a spot of much interest; so is the military burying-ground, where rest the remains of those who fell near here during the prolonged Seminole war. Under three pyramids of coquina, stuccoed and whitened, are the ashes of Major Dade and one hundred and seven men of his command, who were massacred by Osceola and his band. A fine sea-wall of nearly a mile in length, built of coquina with a coping of granite, protects the entire ocean front of the city, and furnishes a delightful promenade of a moonlight evening. In full view of this is the old light-house on Anastasia Island, built more than a century ago, and now surmounted with a fine revolving lantern.

"The street names, Cuna, St. Hypolita, Tolomato, St. George's, and the like, have an ancient and a foreign smack about them; while the family names, such as Dumas, Fatio, Hernandez, Oliverez, Alveres, Monardi, Segui, Andrea, Sanchez, Medices, and Bravo, mark it as any thing but American in its origin. Some of the Roman Catholic customs of carnival and evening serenades before Easter are still kept up by the Minorcan population."

"A word as to these people, who constitute no inconsiderable portion of the present population of St. Augustine. While Florida was in possession of the English, a Dr. Turnbull went to Greece, and received permission to transport such families as chose to go to Florida. Obtaining a small number, not enough for his proposed colony, he halted at the Islands of Corsica and Minorca in the

Mediterranean, where over a thousand joined his company. They landed just inside of Mosquito Inlet, at New Smyrna, some seventy-five miles south of St. Augustine. Turnbull soon became imperious, and by the aid of a few immediate friends reduced these patient, hard-working people to a state of slavery, assigning them tasks under overseers, and treating them in the most shameful manner. His promises of lands and creature comforts, made at the time of their joining his expedition, were disregarded, and with acquired wealth came added austerity and hardships for these now dependent people. Thus for nine years they were in bondage, when, stung to resistance, they assembled clandestinely, and marched in a body to St. Augustine, where they were kindly received, and allowed to remain. They form a very quiet class, attentive to their own affairs, and never meddling with their neighbors. They are intelligent and industrious, and some have acquired considerable property.

"There are a few fine residences in St. Augustine; and these, with their ample surround-

THE ST. AUGUSTINE HOTEL, ST. AUGUSTINE, FLORIDA.

To face p. 112.

ings and beautiful gardens, give a heightened interest to the place. Senator Gilbert has a summer residence here, the first as you enter the town, by the bridge, on the right; then Buckingham Smith's, nearly opposite, and Dr. Bronson's on the plaza, with others, are beautiful homes. A profusion of tropical plants, and shrubs, and trees, ornament their grounds. Here the orange flourishes, and is abundant and delicious: several fine groves invite the visitor's inspection. The fig, and date, and palm, and banana, are all seen here, as also the lime and lemon, which grow to a great size, and the sweet and wild olive; the citron, the guava (from which a delicious jelly is made), and the pomegranate, are all indigenous. This is the home of the grape, and peaches luxuriate in this climate, as likewise the Japan plum.

" Besides the gardens spoken of, we see few flowers; and this is what quite astonishes us in this "land of flowers," where they grow so easily, and with so little care that there seems no excuse why *all* the gardens should not have these simple yet beautiful adornings.

"For many years the town has been at a standstill, and property at a low figure. Good titles can with difficulty be obtained; and this is now the great drawback to the improvement of the place, though within a few years Northern people have been coming in and taking such titles as were offered. One gentleman, Mr. Howard, from New York, has within a year past invested near fifty thousand dollars in real estate in the city, which is beginning to feel the effects of this healthful influx, property having already risen to fourfold its value five years ago, and still not high. The residence of Senator Gilbert, before alluded to, was bought by him at the close of the war, as we are informed, for about eight thousand dollars, and we judge worth forty now. This place has several acres of ground in it.

"The longer one remains in this antique town, the more he is attached to it: at least, this was our experience. It improves on acquaintance. The plaza, or public square, affords a pleasant retreat from the sand, which everywhere else covers the place. Here are

SEA WALL.—ST. AUGUSTINE, FLORIDA.

(To face p. 115.)

shade-trees, and the firm green turf and benches, whereon the visitor may lounge and idle away the hours. At the foot of the square, which fronts on the bay, is the market-house, so entirely different from those elsewhere seen; being here neat, airy, and attractive. It consists of a roof supported by brick pillars, a half-dozen on either side, with a floor of the same material, and is altogether unique in appearance.

"The number of strangers here greatly exceeded our expectations, and thronged in every street and public place. The fashionable belle of Newport and Saratoga, and the pale, thoughtful, and furloughed clergyman of New England, were at all points encountered. The meeting of friends whom we had not seen for years, and others whom we had never met, but yet could call our name, seemed strange and quite a dream."

OCKLAWAHA RIVER.

At Palatka, the tourist to Florida will do well to call upon Captain Adams, the gentlemanly agent of the Dictator and City Point, —from him he can leârn how best to employ his time, and which are the most interesting points to visit. Should the visitor decide upon taking a trip on the Ocklawaha, he will be certain to enjoy a most novel excursion; of late the number desiring to visit this romantic stream has so increased, that the owners of the steamers have felt authorized to increase their passenger accommodations, and we believe they are now quite good.

The following excellent description of a trip on the Ocklawaha is from Appleton's Picturesque America, which contains the most faithful scenes of Florida that have ever been portrayed:

"A sail of twenty miles along the St. John's brought us, a little before sunrise, to the mouth of the Ocklawaha River, looking scarcely wide enough to admit a skiff, much less a steamboat. As daylight increased, we found that we were passing through a dense cypress-swamp, and that the channel selected had no banks, but was indicated by "blazed" marks on the trunks of the towering trees. There was plenty of water, however, to float our craft, but it was a queer kind of navigation, for the hull of the steamer went bumping against one cypress-butt, then another, suggesting to the tyro in this kind of aquatic adventure that possibly he might be wrecked, and subjected, even if he escaped a watery grave, to a miserable death, through the agency of mosquitoes, buzzards, and huge alligators.

As we wound along through the dense vegetation, a picture of novel interest presented itself at every turn. We came occasionally to a spot a little elevated above the dead-water level, covered with a rank growth of lofty palmetto, the very opposite, in every respect, to those stunted, storm-blown specimens which greeted us at the mouth of the St. John's River. Here they shot up tall and slender, bearing aloft innumerable parasites, often surprising the eye with patches, of a half-mile in length, of the convolvulus, in a solid mass of beautiful blossoms.

Another sharp turn, and the wreck of an old dead cypress is discovered, its huge limbs covered with innumerable turkey-buzzards, which are waiting patiently for the decomposition of an alligator that some successful sportsman has shot, and left for the prey of these useful but disgusting birds. The sunshine sparkles in the spray which our awkward yet efficient craft drives from its prow, and then we enter what seems to be a cavern, where the sun never penetrates. The tree-tops interlace, and the tangled vines and innumerable parasites have made a solid mass overhead.

The swamps of Florida are as rich in birds as in vegetation. It is no wonder that Audubon here found one of the finest fields from which to enrich his great works of natural history. A minute list of the varieties we sometimes saw in a single day would fill a page. One of the most attractive was the water-turkey, or snake-bird, which was everywhere to be met with, sitting upon some projecting limb overlooking the water, the body as carefully as possible concealed from view, its head and long neck projecting out, and moving constantly like a black snake in search of its prey. Your curiosity is excited; you would examine the creature more critically, and you fire, at what seems a short, point-blank shot. The bird falls, apparently helpless, in the water; you row rapidly to secure your prize, when, a hundred yards ahead, you suddenly see the snaky head of the "darter" just protruding above the surface of the water. In an instant its lungs are filled with air, and, disappearing again, it reaches a place of safety.

Another conspicuous bird is the large white crane. It is a very effective object in the deep shadows of the cypress, as it proudly stalks about, eyeing with fantastic look the finny tribes it hunts for prey. Especially is it of service in seizing upon the young of the innumerable water-snakes which everywhere abound. With commendable taste, it seems to pay especial attention to the disgusting, slimy, juvenile moccasins, which have a taste for sunning themselves on harsh dried leaves of the stinted palmetto.

But the prominent living object to the stranger in these out-of-the way places is the alligator, whose paradise is in the swamps of Florida. Here he finds a climate that almost the year round suits his delicate constitution; and, while his kindred in the Louisiana swamps find it necessary to retire into the mud to escape the cold of winter, the Florida representative of the tribe is happy in the enjoyment of the upper world the year round. It was a comical and a provoking sight to see these creatures, when indisposed to get out of our way, turn up their piggish eyes in speculative mood at the sudden interruption of a rifle-ball against their mailed sides, but all the while seemingly unconscious that any harm against their persons was intended. Like Achilles, however, they possess a vulnerable point, which is just in front of the spot where the huge head works upon the spinal column. There is, of necessity, at this place a joint in the armor, and a successful hunter, after much experience, seldom lets one of the reptiles escape. If any philanthropist has ever objected to the slaughter, the circumstance is not remembered in the swamps and everglades of Florida. On one occasion we fired into a herd of alligators, and the noise of two or three shots caused all but one to finally disappear. For some reason it seemed difficult to get the remaining one to move, the creature lying with its head exposed to our gaze, looking as demoniac as possible. A bullet, which struck somewhere in the vicinity of its jaws, touched its feelings, and then, with a grunt not unlike that of a hog, it buried itself in the muddy water. This unwillingness to move was then explained by the appearance of a large number of young alligators, which, in the confusion, came to the surface like so many chips. We had, without being aware of it, attacked the mother while she was protecting her nest.

In the vicinity of the alligator's nest we came upon a primitive post-office, consisting of a cigar-box, bearing the magic letters "U. S. M.," nailed upon the face of an old cypress-tree. It was a sort of central point for the swampers, where they left their soiled notes and crooked writing to be conveyed to the places of destination by "whomever came along." We, desiring to act the part of a volunteer mail-carrier for the neighbourhood, peeped into the post-office, but there were no signs of letters; so our good intentions were of no practical effect.

Our little nondescript craft bumps along from one cypress-stump, and fetches up against a *cypress-knee*, as it is termed—sharp-pointed lances which grow up from the roots of the trees, seemingly to protect the trunk from too much outside concussion; glancing off, it runs into a roosting-place of innumerable cranes, or scatters the wild ducks and huge snakes over the surface of the water. A clear patch of the sky is seen, and the bright light of a summer evening is tossing the feathery crowns of the old cypress-trees into a nimbus of glory, while innumerable paroquets, alarmed at our intrusion, scream out their fierce indignation, and then, flying away, flash upon our admiring eyes their green and golden plumage. It now begins to grow dark in earnest, and we become curious to know how our attentive pilot will safely navigate this mysterious channel in what is literally Egyptian darkness. While thus speculating, there flashes across the landscape a bright, clear light. From the most intense blackness we have a fierce, lurid glare, presenting the most extravagantly-picturesque groups of overhanging palmettos, draped with parasites and vines of all descriptions; prominent among the latter is the scarlet trumpet-creeper, overburdened with wreaths of blossoms, and intertwined again with chaplets of purple and white convolvulus, the most minute details of the objects near being brought out in a sharp red light against the deep tone of the forest's depths. But no imagination can conceive the grotesque and wierd forms which constantly force themselves on your notice as the light partially illuminates the limbs of wrecked or half-destroyed trees, which, covered with moss, or wrapped in decayed vegetation as a winding-sheet, seem huge unburied monsters, which, though dead, still throw about their arms in agony, and gaze through unmeaning eyes upon the intrusions of active, living men.

Another run of a half-mile brings us into the cypress again, the firelight giving new ideas of the picturesque. The tall shafts, more than ever shrouded in the hanging moss, look as if they had been draped in sad habiliments, while the wind sighed through the limbs; and when the sonorous sounds of the alligators were heard, groaning and complaining, the sad, dismal picture of desolation was complete.

A sharp contact with a palmetto-knee throws round the head of our nondescript steamer, and we enter what appears to be an endless colonnade of beautifully-proportioned shafts, running upward a hundred feet, roofed by pendent ornaments, suggesting the highest possible effect of Gothic architecture. The delusion was increased by the waving streamers of the Spanish moss, which here and there, in great festoons of fifty feet in length, hung down like tattered but gigantic banners, worm-eaten and mouldy, sad evidences of the hopes and passions of the distant past. So absorbing were these wonderful effects of a brilliant light upon the vegetable productions of these Florida swamps, that we had forgotten to look for the cause of this artificial glare, but, when we did, we found a faithful negro had suspended from cranes two iron cages, one on each side of the boat, into which he constantly placed unctuous pine-knots, that blazed and crackled, and turned what would otherwise have been unmeaning darkness into the most novel and exciting views of Nature that ever met our experienced eyes.

The morning came, and the theatrical display of the swamp by torchlight ended, when we were destined to be introduced to a new feature of this singular navigation. A huge water-oak, seemingly in the very pride of its matured existence, had fallen directly across the channel. Its wood was only a little less hard than iron, and the labor to be performed to get this obstruction out of the way was contemplated with anger by the captain of our craft, and in sadness by the "hands," to whose lot fell the labor of clearing the obstruction away. However, the order was given, and no inhabitant of the swamp is inexperienced in the use of the axe. The sturdy blows fell thick and fast, as one limb after another broke loose from the parent trunk and floated slowly away. The great butt was then assailed, and, by a judicious choice in the assault, the weight of the huge structure was made to assist in breaking it in twain. While this work was going on, which consumed some hours, we waded—we won't say ashore—but, from one precarious foothold to another, until, after various unpleasant experiences—the least of which was getting wet to our waist in the black water of the swamp—we reached land, which was a few inches above the surface of the prevailing flood.

We were, however, rewarded for our enterprise, by suddenly coming upon two "Florida crackers," who had established a camp in a grove of the finest cypress-trees we ever saw, and were appropriating the valuable timber to the manufacture of shingles, which shingles, we were informed, are almost as indestructible as slate. These men were civil, full of character, and, in their way, not wanting in intelligence. How they manage to survive the discomforts of their situation is difficult to imagine, but they do exist; the mosquitoes drawing from their bodies every useless drop of blood, the low swamp malaria making the accumulation of fat an impossibility, while the dull surroundings of their life, to them most monotonous, cramp the intellect, until they are almost as taciturn as the trees with which they are associated. But their hut was a very model of the picturesque; and the smouldering fire, over which their dinner-pot was cooking, sent up a wreath of blue smoke against the dark openings of the deep forest that gave a quiet charm, and a contrast of colors, difficult to sufficiently admire, and impossible to be conceived of in the mere speculations of studio life.

One of our strangest experiences in these mysterious regions was forced upon us one morning, when, thrusting our head through the hole that gave air to our "sleeping-shelf," we saw a sight which caused us to rub our eyes, and gather up our senses, to be certain we were positively awake. Our rude craft was in a basin possibly a quarter of a mile in diameter, entirely surrounded by gigantic forest-trees, which repeated themselves with the most minute fidelity in the perfectly translucent water. For sixty feet downward we could look, and at this great depth see duplicated the scene of the upper world; the clearness of the water assisting rather than interfering with the vision. The bottom of this basin was silver sand, studded with pale emeralds, eccentric formations of lime-crystals—a bed of white coral in forms and color that reminded us of the cunningly-wrought silver baskets of Genoa. This, we soon learned, was the wonderful silver spring of which we had heard so much, which every moment throws out its thousands of gallons of water without making a bubble on the surface.

Procuring a "dug-out," provided with a gun, and furnished with our drawing-materials, and a lunch that would answer for the day, we deliberately proceeded to inform ourself of the mysteries of the spot. The transparency of the water was ever a constant wonder. A little pearly white shell, dropped from our hand, worked its zigzag way downward, becoming in its descent a mere emerald tint, until, finding the bottom, it seemed to be a gem destined forever to glisten in its silver setting.

Noticing the faintest possible movement on the surface of the basin at a certain point, we concluded that that must be over the place where the great body of the water entered the spring. So, paddling to the spot, and wrapping a stone weighing about eight ounces in a piece of white paper, we dropped it into the water at the place where the slightly perceptible movement was visible. The stone went perpendicularly down for some twenty-five feet, until it reached a slight projection of limestone rock, where it was suddenly, as if a feather in weight, forced upward in a curving line some fifteen feet, showing the tremendous power of the water that rushes out from the rock buried under this bed of burning sand. Perhaps the most novel and startling feature was when our craft came from the shade into the sunshine, for then, looking over the sides of the canoe, we recoiled at the sensation of *floating in the air.* For it seemed as if we were, by some miraculous power, suspended seventy feet or more in the mid air, while down on the sanded bottom was a sharp, clear *silhouette* of man, boat, and paddle. A deep river a hundred feet wide is created by the water of this spring, which, in the course of seven miles, forms a junction with the Ocklawaha, and then continues to run side by side for another mile, without mixing its clear, pellucid water with the coffee-stained flow of the other stream, which, like most of the rivers of Florida, is heavily charged with alluvial and vegetable matter.

Such are some of the wonders of the land discovered by Ponce de Leon.

INDIAN RIVER.

The sportsman can charter a Minorcan vessel at St. Augustine, on reasonable terms, to carry him to the famous Indian River; or, he can, if he prefers it, go up the St. John's to Enterprise, and so reach the river.

The writer of this work does not propose to endorse any fish story, but to give an idea of the sport in Indian River, gives the following extracts from the letter of a correspondent of the New York *Sun*, written last spring; the account is not an exaggeration, for it is simply impossible to exaggerate the variety or quantity of fish to be found in this wonderful inlet:

"The gamest fish in Florida is the channel bass or red-fish. It is a salt water fish, built like a striped bass. It has silvery and red golden scales, but no stripes. A round mother-of-pearl spot on the neck of the tail is its most striking mark. Channel bass hang about the mouths of fresh water brooks in great swarms at certain seasons of the year, and gobble up the young mullet. In the fall of the year the mullet is a delicious fish. It never takes the hook, but is caught in a cast-net.

WONDERS OF THE CAST-NET.

"Every sea-coast family in Florida below

St. Augustine owns a cast-net. Spread upon the grass this net is about twenty feet in circumference. The edge is loaded with heavy sliding sinkers, each of which fills the outer stitch of the net. From the center runs a strong cord from eighteen to thirty feet in length. The thrower takes the end of this cord between his teeth, arranges the net in folds on his right arm, firmly seizes a fold in each hand, swings himself partly around, and then gives the net a powerful heave. It strikes the water in a circle, the sinkers instantly carry the rim to the bottom, and every fish beneath it is a prisoner. The fisherman then draws in the net by a cord, while the weight of the sinkers brings them together, thus preventing the escape of the fish. The art of throwing the net is acquired only by constant practice. It looks easy enough, but there is a knack about it that renders it difficult. I have seen a twelve year boy send it eighteen feet, when a two-hundred-pound greenhorn could not even spread it on the water. An adept will throw it from twenty to thirty feet.

GREEN CATFISH—CHANNEL BASS.

"I caught my first channel bass at Turtle Mound on a Cuddyhunk hook, which was much too small. Standing upon the point of a spit of sand, I cast the mullet-baited hook fifty feet into the water. Five minutes passed before a bite. The fish was fastened and reeled in. It was a two-pound cat-fish of a delicate green color. In the sun it had the lustre of a green silk dress. A second time I drew in a green cat-fish. Then half an hour elapsed without a bite. I grew discouraged, and running the line from the reel, walked back to a bunch of stunted palmettos and laid my rod across them, intending to go to the sea beach and look for shells. I had gone nearly two hundred feet, when I looked back and saw the reel running out at smoking speed. The rod had started over the sand before I reached it. The fish was evidently a large one, and wanted play. He ran up and down the river as though he had been dosed with laughing gas. It was ten minutes before he became quiet, and I began to work the reel. When within twenty feet of the shore he made a second break, taking two hundred feet of line. I could feel him shaking his head and trying to get the hook out of his mouth as he sped away. Then he ran in upon me like a race-horse, faster than I could take in the slack. Dashing into the shallow water, he took a look at his tormentor. It was not satisfactory. Making a wide sweep, he flirted the foam into my face with his tail, and again sailed off into the river, raising a swell upon the surface of the water. For an instant he was quiet, and then there was a circus-horse performance, which lasted over a minute. Finally the fish became exhausted, and was cautiously reeled in. I had no gaff-hook, and was about to stick my fingers into his gills and draw him upon the sand, when Dr. Fox, my guide, said, 'Catch him under the fore fins; he's got teeth in his gills.' I found two pockets or arm-pits under his fins, and pulled him ashore. He was a channel bass, weighing twenty-two pounds. Within twenty minutes I took in a second one, weighing a little short of fourteen pounds.

At Seventy, near Pepper Hammock, I caught a twenty-five-pound fellow.

THE PRINCE OF FEATHERED GLUTTONS.

" The pelican is the prince of feathered gluttons. I shot a dozen of them on the wing. Sometimes the fish would begin to tumble out of their gullets before they reached the ground. In no case did I find less than four large fish in their baggy throats. The lower fish would be half digested. Their throttles are like mill hoppers. They fill the pouch under their bill with a peck of fish. The fish overflow into their throats. As fast as one digests another drops into its place, and goes through the same process. The bird is fat, logy, and very rank. It is full of grease. Handle a dead one in the sun or before a camp fire, and the grease will drop from the body. They weigh from twelve to twenty pounds. Dr. Fox shot a white one measuring nine feet and one inch from tip to tip, and weighing nineteen and three-quarters pounds. While sitting upon the water they hold their heads well up, with their enormous bills and pouches flattened upon their breasts. They look as grave as country judges—so grave that but few persons can see them without laughing outright. They fly in Indian file, sometimes in strings half a mile long. When the leader flaps his wings the second one follows suit, and so on down the line; and when the leader soars number two does the same, and is followed by the others. Each bird seems to be under strict discipline, and when gathered in great flocks upon the beach they resemble an army massed by battalions. The plumage of the grey pelican is much admired. Every feather is shaded from a black to a beautiful silver grey. The under part of the neck resembles yellow satin, and the back part is a glossy brown velvet.

THE HIGHWAY ROBBERS OF THE AIR.

"It is amusing to watch an osprey while he is fishing. An eagle is soaring through the air five hundred feet above him. The osprey is sailing over the water, carefully eyeing its surface. Suddenly he steadies himself against the wind, rolling his wings as though endeavoring to back water. Then he drops through the air like a plummet. There is a splash in the waves, and the osprey rises with a fish in his talons. Meanwhile the eagle is drawing near. As the osprey ascends in the air, the eagle utters a threatening cry and swoops upon him. Unable to escape, the hawk finally drops the fish. Before it strikes the water the eagle darts downward like a flash of lightning and catches it, while the osprey flies to a hammock, where his comrades gather round and sympathize with him.

THE DANCING FISH.

"A man-of-war hawk or frigate pelican is a peculiar fisherman. He descends upon his prey like a bullet from a height of three hundred feet. He seizes the fish in his beak, and soars aloft into the sky. His mates gather about him, while the lucky fisherman tosses his tidbit into the air so as to catch it by the head, and swallow it, as it comes down. His throat is so small that he can get it in his stomach in no other way. There is a wild swoop, and another hawk seizes the fish, and again it is tossed in the air, and tossed up indefinitely, until one of the birds is so fortunate as to catch it head-first, when it disappears. I have seen a dozen frigate pelicans keep a fish dancing in the air fifteen minutes before it was swallowed.

"The most wonderful fishermen on the Indian River is a native named Stewart. He seems to be amphibious. It is no uncommon thing for him to jump into the water and run down a fat mullet, catching it in his hands. The Futch family have two dogs so starved that I have seen them dash into a school of mullet and reappear with fish in their mouths.

FISH CAUGHT IN FLORIDA.

"Among the fish caught at Smyrna are sheepshead, bass or red-fish, the red and black grouper, salt water trout, mullet, king-fish (the natives call it whiting), sea-bass, pig-fish, drum-fish, sailor's choice or porgie, sergeant-fish, cavallo, snapjack or blue-fish, green and black cat-fish, red and black snappers, menatee, lady-fish, jew-fish, stingarees, sharks, dog-fish, porpoises, saw-fish, sword-fish, ribbon-fish, pompaneau, different kinds of cuttle fish, two kinds of eels, (natives call them congarees,) an electrical flounder, similar to an electrical eel, flukes, skates, big shrimps, whipparees, or clam-crackers, bezonga, toad-fish, blow-fish, porcupine fish, cow-fish, mojarra, angel-fish and spade-fish.

"The grouper is a sort of a salt-water perch, and is highly prized for its flavor and gameness. It is generally caught in deep water.

"The salt-water trout is not the Northern weak-fish. It resembles a brook trout, but the dots on its sides are black, and not red. It bites like a weak-fish, and is game to the backbone.

"The pig-fish is built like a grouper. It is a game fish, and derives its name from the fact that it grunts like a pig when thrown from the hook to the bottom of the boat.

"The sheepshead are not so large as Northern fish of this name.

"The sergeant-fish is a salt-water pike. It is a splendid fighter, and is called a sergeant-fish because it has three stripes running across its body similar to a sergeant's chevrons. It grows as large as a muscalonge.

"The cavallo or 'crevalyea,' is a favorite game fish. Its head and fins are tipped with gold. The former is shaped like the prow of an old-fashioned Erie canal boat. The fish is very narrow at the root of the tail, which has a golden tinge.

"The lady-fish is delicate and silvery. When struck by the hook they spring from the water with more energy than a black bass. Their flavor is delicious.

"The jew-fish grows to an enormous size, occasionally reaching five hundred pounds in weight. It is of a greenish color, covered with irregular dark spots, and is very game. Why it is called a jew-fish is one of those things that no person can find out.

"The saw-fish becomes very large, and takes the hook like an old stager. A flat bone, set with teeth on either edge, juts from its nose, giving the fish its name. It is good eating and game.

"The ribbon-fish has a snout like a pike. It is a thin fish, strung out like a ribbon, from which it takes its name. It is regarded as a delicacy.

"Stingarees are plentiful, and of an enormous size. Some of them weigh two hundred and fifty pounds. The sting is in their tail. It is a bone several inches in length, bearded in a hundred places like the shank of a hook. The fish can throw it through a man's boot, or even through his body. It is a dangerous fish, and has been known to cause death in a few hours. The natives use the stingaree's tail for toothpicks. They declare that it prevents toothache.

"The pompeneau is the pride of Southern epicures. It is caught in a net, and has a round body, shining like a plate of silver. Its bones are soft, and it has a flavor superior to that of a shad.

A FISH THAT EATS GRASS.

"The menatee, or sea-cow, is a huge amphibious animal. It is found in the St. Lucie River. It has a head like that of a sea-lion, and it looks like a gigantic seal. It feeds upon the rank grass growing upon the marshes of the St. Lucie. The menatee has ribs as thick as a man's arm. Last year Dolph Sheldon and Frank Sams caught one alive near the mouth of the river, intending to send it North for exhibition. The animal weighed over one thousand five hundred pounds. Unfortunately it was tied to the boat so firmly that the rope cut into its flesh, and it died before the party reached the head of Indian River. The porgies devoured the body. Florida is the only place in which the menatee is found on the North American continent. Formerly it was abundant, but it is now nearly extinct, and becomes more scarce every year. Its meat is greatly relished, and tastes like the best Fulton Market beef.

"The whipparee resembles the stingaree. Its mouth is filled with two ivory rocks, and between them it cracks the clams on which it feeds. It reaches an enormous size.

"The porcupine-fish has a round body filled with quills. It is small, and good for nothing.

"The cow-fish is a curious fish. It has the

head of a pig, with two horns above the ears. On the bottom it is as smooth as a flat-iron.

"The mojarra is the shape of a sheepshead, and has a lustrous brown shading above the tail. It is as handsome as an angel-fish, and is good eating.

"The spade-fish also looks like a sheepshead, but it has no hard fins.

NO TROUT IN FLORIDA.

"All the books on Florida declare that the rivers are filled with trout. This is untrue. There is not a fresh-water trout in the State. What they call trout are a kind of black bass, trapped on a troll. They have huge mouths, and are caught by scores in the St. John's River. A lady hooked one at Enterprise weighing ten pounds and a half. Compared with sea fishing, however, fishing on the St. John is boyish sport.

EXCURSIONS.

From St. Augustine and Enterprise, many excursions can be made, with perfect safety, into an almost unexplored region abounding in fish and game; and one's time—whether in a sojourn of a few weeks, or during an entire winter—be most agreeably occupied in Florida.

There are many quite important points in Florida, in a business point of view, not touched upon in this work; but we believe we have here given all that interests the general reader, or the seeker after health or recreation in relation to Florida.

FINIS.

FOR FLORIDA, THE

First-Class New-York Built Steamers

DICTATOR, - Capt. Vogel,
CITY POINT, - Capt. Fitzgerald,

Connect at CHARLESTON and SAVANNAH with the New York Steamers and Northern Trains for

SAVANNAH, | *HIBERNIA,*
FERNANDINA, | *MAGNOLIA,*
JACKSONVILLE, | *GREEN COVE Springs,*
St. AUGUSTINE, | *PALATKA,*

INCLUDING ALL LANDINGS ON THE ST. JOHN'S RIVER.

CONNECT AT PALATKA WITH STEAMERS FOR ENTERPRISE, MELLONVILLE, SANFORD, AND INDIAN RIVER. ALSO WITH STEAMERS FOR THE OCKLAWAHA RIVER.

A sufficient number of the CHOICEST STATE-Rooms are reserved for Passengers by the NEW YORK STEAMERS.

Passengers will find on these Steamers every comfort and convenience— a first-class table, and polite and attentive employees.

For Freight or passage, apply in New York to Agents of Charleston and Savannah Steamship Lines.

The DICTATOR and CITY POINT

have during the Summer been elegantly refurnished, and put in the most thorough order, nothing being left undone to provide every comfort and convenience. The traveler will bear in mind they land him at the very doors of the following hotels, without change of conveyance.

SAVANNAH.

PULASKI HOUSE, SCREVEN HOUSE, PAVILION HOTEL and MARSHALL HOUSE.

FERNANDINA.

RIDELL HOUSE, and numerous BOARDING HOUSES.

JACKSONVILLE.

INTERNATIONAL, ST. JAMES' HOTEL, METROPOLITAN HOTEL, ST. JOHN'S HOUSE Mrs. DAY'S, Mrs. ATKIN'S, Mrs. STOCKTON'S and Mrs. BUFFINGTON'S.

HIBERNIA.

Mrs. FLEMING'S.

GREEN COVE SPRINGS.

UNION HOTEL and CLARENDON HOTEL.

THE HOTEL AT MAGNOLIA.

PALATKA.

ST. JOHN'S HOTEL and PUTNAM HOTEL.

At Tocoi landing passengers at the Cars for **St. Augustine,** taking them direct to ST. AUGUSTINE HOTEL, MAGNOLIA HOUSE, and the numerous BOARDING HOUSES of the Ancient City.

Connecting at PALATKA with Steamers taking the passengers to BROCK'S HOTEL, ENTERPRISE, and the various BOARDING HOUSES at MELLONVILLE.

By this direct communication the traveler is saved great perplexity and trouble.

All Through Railroad Tickets

TO

FLORIDA

RECEIVED ON THESE

Steamers in Payment of Passage,

AND

NO EXTRA CHARGE

IS MADE

For Meals or State-Rooms.

An attentive Stewardess is charged with the care of LADIES and CHILDREN, whose duty it is to see them provided with every comfort.

Each Steamer is provided with a well-filled Medicine Chest, and the attendants, accustomed to the wants of invalids, will at all times be found cheerfully to give their assistance when called upon.

These Steamers being heated by Steam, a pleasant uniform temperature is maintained during the Winter Months in Saloons and State-Rooms.

Whether pleasure-seekers or invalids, will find the route by the DICTATOR and CITY POINT the most enjoyable and the least expensive; it is the only route by which the beautiful scenery of the lower ST. JOHN'S RIVER can be viewed, with the many points rendered interesting, as the scenes of the earliest settlements on the Continent, and of the many bloody struggles between the French and Spaniards.

Those traveling with invalids—ladies or children, will particularly appreciate the trouble and anxiety avoided, by being carried direct to their destination without several times having to shift baggage, etc., etc.

The steamers are of the safest description, especially adapted to the service—fitted with every comfort and convenience—clean, comfortable State Rooms, a table provided with every luxury of the Charleston, Savannah and Florida markets, and equal to that of any first-class hotel.

The DICTATOR and CITY POINT are commanded by officers who have spent their lives in the Florida trade, and they, as well as all the employees on the Steamers, will take pleasure in giving every information to visitors, and to those intending to settle in Florida.

Goods and Packages will be forwarded by the Agents, free of commission.

RAVENEL & CO., Agents,
Charleston, South Carolina.

For Speed, Safety and Comfort,

TAKE THE GREAT

SOUTHERN FREIGHT,
AND
PASSENGER LINE,

FOR CHARLESTON, S. C.,

The Florida Ports,
AND THE
South and South-West,

Sailing from Pier 29, North River, at 3 p. m., every

TUESDAY, THURSDAY AND SATURDAY.

Through Passage Tickets and Bills of Lading issued at lowest rates.

FOR LOCAL FREIGHT AND PASSAGE TO ALL POINTS,
APPLY TO
JAMES W. QUINTARD & CO.,
177 West Street, cor. Warren.

FOR THROUGH FREIGHT TARIFF AND RATES
APPLY TO
BENTLEY D. HASELL,
General Agent Great Southern Freight Line,
317 BROADWAY.

IMPORTANT TO TRAVELERS TO FLORIDA.

The Magnificent Side-Wheel Steamships

MANHATTAN,	M. S. Woodhull,	Commander.
CHAMPION,	R. W. Lockwood,	"
CHARLESTON,	James Berry,	"
JAMES ADGER,	T. J. Lockwood,	"
GEORGIA,	Holmes,	"
SOUTH CAROLINA,	Crowell,	"

Leave New York for Charleston, S. C.,

EVERY

Tuesday, Thursday & Saturday,

AT 3 O'CLOCK P.M., FROM PIER 29 N. R.

connecting with the Charleston and Florida steamships "DICTATOR" and "CITY POINT" for Jacksonville, St. Augustine, and other points in Florida.

This is the shortest and pleasantest sea route. Travelers have the option of remaining in Charleston at their convenience, and reviewing the historic

RUINS OF FORT SUMTER,

and other points of interest in and around Charleston. These steamships also connect with the trains on the South-Carolina Railroad for AIKEN, S. C., AUGUSTA, Ga., and all points south.

THROUGH TICKETS TO ALL POINTS IN FLORIDA, SOUTH CAROLINA, GEORGIA, ALABAMA, AND TENNESSEE MAY BE OBTAINED AT THE OFFICE OF THE NEW YORK AGENTS.

JAMES W. QUINTARD & Co.,   **JAMES ADGER & CO.,**

117 West St., Cor. Warren.   Agents at Charleston, S. Carolina.

GREAT SOUTHERN FREIGHT

AND

Passenger Route,

VIA

SAVANNAH, Ga,

FOR

FLORIDA,

AND ALL

POINTS in the SOUTH and SOUTH-WEST.

One of the following First-Class Steamships will sail every other day as follows,—punctually at 3 o'clock, p. m. :

EVERY TUESDAY,

From Pier 16, E. R., foot of Wall St.,

LEO & VIRGO, of Murray's Line,

MURRAY, FERRIS & Co., Agents, 61 and 62 South St.

EVERY THURSDAY,

From Pier 43, N. R.

HERMAN LIVINGSTON & GEN. BARNES.

EVERY SATURDAY,

From Pier 43, N. R.

SAN SALVADOR & SAN JACINTO,

W. R. GARRISON, Agent, 5 Bowling Green.

Making close connections at Savannah, with Central R. R., Ga; Atlantic and Gulf R. R., and Steamboats for St. John's River and Florida.

WILLIAM M. BIRD & CO.,

OILS,

White Leads,

Zincs, Colors,

WINDOW GLASS, Etc.

No. 201 East Bay Street, Charleston, S. C.,

AND

No. 8 Whitaker Street, Savannah, Ga.

Charleston Hotel,
CHARLESTON, S. Carolina.

This well-known and popular first-class Hotel, situated in the Centre of the City, and also in the centre of the Wholesale Business Houses, affords facilities, comforts and attention to Travelers for pleasure, and Merchants on business, second to none in the United States.

Having been recently thoroughly repaired and newly furnished throughout, the Proprietor pledges himself to spare no pains in its management to maintain the high reputation heretofore enjoyed by the old **CHARLESTON** *as a first-class house.*

E. H. JACKSON, Prop'r.

General Railway and Steamship Ticket Office. Through Tickets sold by Rail to all points in the United States, and by Rail or Steamship to **Baltimore, Philadelphia** *and* **New York.**

A. BUTTERFIELD, General Ticket Agent,
CHARLESTON HOTEL.

Pavilion Hotel,

CHARLESTON, S. C.

This house, having been newly furnished and painted throughout, and having the *Celebrated Artesian Water* introduced on every floor, is now open for the reception of guests. The apartments are spacious, well ventilated, and thoroughly adapted to the comfort of the traveling public.

ARTESIAN BATHS having been established in connection with this house, makes it particularly desirable for INVALIDS, and the traveling public generally.

The proprietors have spared neither trouble nor expense in the renovation of the CULINARY department.

A FIRST-CLASS LIVERY STABLE is connected with the Hotel, and Omnibuses and Carriages for the conveyance of passengers, will be in attendance at all the Steamboat Landings and Rail-road Depots.

The Proprietors would respectfully ask a share of public patronage, promising to give satisfaction.

GEO. T. ALFORD & CO., Proprietors.

Pulaski House,

SAVANNAH, GEORGIA.

 This well-known hotel, which has always been considered the leading hotel in Savannah, and one of the best in the South, is pleasantly located in the central portion of the city, on Johnson Square, with a southern front, which is a matter of no small importance in this climate. In consequence of the death of the late proprietor, Major W. H. WILTBERGER, the hotel has fallen into the hands of Messrs. S. N. PAPOT & Co., and the new proprietors have made many changes and improvements. The whole house has been thoroughly painted inside and out, and otherwise renovated; and such alterations have been made in the interior arrangements, as must add to its attractions and conduce to the comfort of the guests.

 At this hotel every convenience is offered to the traveling public in the way of Ticket Offices for all the Railroads and Steamboats; Telegraph Office, etc., and here also Sleeping-car tickets can be procured. A handsome billiard-room has been provided for the use of the guests, which we are induced to mention, as it is a thing which has been long wanted, and as it is the only hotel in Savannah which contains any such means of amusement.

 If kind and courteous treatment, comfortable rooms and a good table offer any inducements to our friends going South, either for health, pleasure or business, we think we can safely recommend them to patronise the Pulaski during their sojourn in Savannah.

S. N. PAPOT & CO.,

SCREVEN HOUSE,

SAVANNAH, GA.

The undersigned take pleasure in informing their patrons and the traveling Public generally, that during the past Summer they have thoroughly renovated, re-decorated, and much improved this well-known house.

Every requisite for the comfort and pleasure of their guests has been made.

The location is deemed one of the best and healthiest in the city—fronting on a public square.

The Cuisine has been particularly attended to, and the services of the best French cooks secured.

Bath-rooms have been recently fitted up for the use of guests.

The House is still under the same proprietorship as last year, assisted by Mr. I. W. Tuttle, who has been long connected with the establishment.

R. BRADLEY & SON,
Proprietors.

PAVILION HOTEL,

Bull Street, cor. South Broad.

SAVANNAH, GA.

—:o:—

A. FERNANDEZ, Proprietor.

—:o:—

BOARD PER DAY, $3; PER WEEK, $15.

The undersigned would respectfully inform his friends and the public generally, that he has leased the Pavilion Hotel, and has put it in complete order, and is now ready to receive Boarders either permanent or transient.

The House is eligibly located on the principal promenade of the city, and is admirably adapted for the purpose for which it is used. Every effort will be made to merit the patronage of the public.

A. FERNANDEZ,
Late of the Pulaski and Screven Houses.

McCONNELL'S
European House,
AND
RESTAURANT,

116 & 118 Bryan Street, Savannah, Ga.

BOARD WITH ROOMS, $2.00 PER DAY; LARGE AIRY SINGLE ROOMS, WITHOUT BOARD, $1.00 PER DAY.

The Restaurant is supplied with all the delicacies of the Northern and Southern Markets.

D. McCONNELL, Proprietor.

RIDDELL HOUSE,

Fernandina, Florida.

Daily Communications with all Parts of the Country,

BY

STEAMER and RAILROAD.

This house is on the Seaboard, in the most healthy part of the State of Florida. The drive of 18 *miles on the most magnificent beach on the Atlantic Coast presents a great attraction to visitors. The excursions in the neighborhood are interesting, particularly that to Cumberland Island, and the well known Dungeness.*

The house has lately been put in thorough repair, and will be found conducted in a most superior style by the proprietor.

SAMUEL T. RIDDELL,

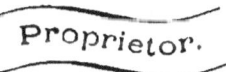
Proprietor.

Banking & Collection Office

OF

D. G. AMBLER,

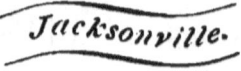
Jacksonville.

DEALER IN

Exchange, Stocks, Bonds, Notes

AND

SPECIE.

Special Attention given to Investments for Capitalists.

Interest Allowed on Deposits.

———...———

Visitors to Florida afforded every possible facility. Drafts on Northern Cities cashed on favorable terms. Every information cheerfully afforded the Tourist or Invalid as to the various Winter Resorts of Florida—routes of travel, etc., etc. Our files of Northern papers may at all times be consulted.

D. G. AMBLER.

THE
ST. JAMES HOTEL,

(Fronting St. James Park,)

Jacksonville, Florida.

OPEN FROM NOVEMBER TO MAY.

THE St. James Hotel has accommodations for 300 guests. Its location is the finest in Florida. A new brick wing, 110 feet by 46 feet, three stories high, with spacious parlors on the first-floor, and large airy sleeping rooms with fire place in each, on the second and third floors, has been added during the past Summer. The entire house has been refurnished in first-class style with sofa-spring beds and best hair mattresses.

Families and others seeking the delightful climate of Florida will find the St. James a comfortable home for the winter.

J. R. CAMPBELL & J. N. ANDREWS,

GENERAL MANAGERS.

Grand National Hotel,

JACKSONVILLE.

GEORGE McGINLEY, PROPRIETOR.

The Grand National, recently completed, is now open for the reception of guests. Its situation is unrivalled, commanding a magnificent view of the St. John's River, and convenient to the steamer landings and railroad depot.

Visitors will find here every comfort, large, finely furnished, and well-ventilated apartments, and an excellent table.

Bath rooms, billiard room, livery stable, etc., attached to hotel. In fact, every requisite of a first-class house.

GEORGE McGINLEY, Proprietor.

Metropolitan Hotel,

Jacksonville, Fla.

Built of Brick,—New Throughout.

Florida Land Agency,

Jacksonville, Fla.

C. L. ROBINSON, Proprietor.

Attorney at Law.—Commissioner U. S. Circuit Court.—Special Commissioner U. S. Court Claims.—Publisher " Florida Land Register."

Mrs. E. HUDNALL, Proprietress.

MRS. BUFFINGTON,

Private Boarding,

JACKSONVILLE, FLA.

GUESTS WILL FIND EVERY COMFORT.

Academy of St. Joseph,

JACKSONVILLE, East Fla.

MOTHER SIDONIER, Sup.

The Sisters of St. Joseph have a separate house for the accommodation of persons desiring to spend the winter.

MRS. S. E. DAY,

JACKSONVILLE, FLA.

Private Boarding,

FORSYTH STREET.

Private Boarding,

AT

Mrs. A. V. C. ATKINS,

MONROE STREET, 1st Door from Market St.,

JACKSONVILLE, EAST FLORIDA.

MRS. STOCKTON,

Private Boarding,

JACKSONVILLE, Fla.

J. B. TOGNI,
Metropolitan Hall,

DEALER IN FOREIGN

Wines, Liquors and Segars;

IMPORTER OF FINE

FRENCH BRANDIES, CLARET and ITALIAN WINES,

Olive Oil, Cordials, Delicacies, Etc.

Excursion Parties fitted out with every requisite for extended trips to the Interior.

Proprietor of the Metropolitan Billiard Saloon, where visitors will find tables of the celebrated makers, both Pocket and Carom. Liquors of our own importation furnished at the bar.

The large Hall in the building can be secured on reasonable terms for Concerts, Theatrical Representations, etc., etc.

J. B. TOGNI.

C. B. McCLENNY'S STABLES

Jacksonville, Fla.,

OPPOSITE SAINT JAMES' & METROPOLITAN HOTELS.

PLEASURE CARRIAGES, OPEN & CLOSE,

To Let, with Careful Drivers.

Horses, Buggies & Saddle-Horses

FURNISHED AT THE SHORTEST NOTICE.

Omnibuses, Hacks and Baggage Wagons meet all Boats and Trains.

Special attention paid to orders left at either Stable for Passengers or Baggage.

DAMON GREENLEAF,

JACKSONVILLE, Fla.,

DEALER IN

Watches, Clocks, Jewelry, Solid Silver,

AND

PLATED WARE.

—:o:—

Watches, Clocks and Jewelry Repaired & Warranted.

—:o:—

HEAD-QUARTERS FOR

FLORIDA CURIOSITIES.

Do not fail while in Florida, to visit Greenleaf's Museum of Florida Curiosities, connected with Greenleaf's Jewelry Store, opposite the Market.

ADMISSION FREE.

Constantly on hand, the largest stock in the State of ca Beans, mounted in every style; Alligator Heads, Alligator Teeth, carved and mounted; Orange, Royal Palm, Palmetto, Break-axe, Mangrove, and other Canes.

Pink Curlew Wings, Egret and Heron Plumes; Flamingo and Fawn Plumes; Sea Shells and Coral; Alligator Eggs, etc., etc.

Sole Agent for the celebrated Bahamian Shell-Work.

Dry and Fancy Goods.

FURCHGOTT, BENEDICT & CO.'S

KNOWN AS THE

TRADE PALACE.

The most beautiful and finest Store in the State.

BAY STREET, Jacksonville, Fla.

Branch of CHARLESTON HOUSE, 275 King St.

New York Office, 86 Leonard Street.

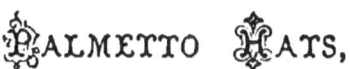
PALMETTO HATS,

Carpets and Matting, a Specialty.

SAMUEL B. HUBBARD,

JACKSONVILLE, Fla.,

IMPORTER AND DEALER IN

Hardware,
    Iron and Steel,
        Edge Tools,
            Table and Pocket Cutlery,
            Nails, Glue,
                Putty, Glass,
Paints, Oils,
    Leather Belting,
        Rubber Packing,
            Stoves, Tinware,
                Crockery, Pumps

LEAD AND IRON PIPE,

DOORS, SASHES, BLINDS, MOULDINGS, SUGAR MILLS, EVAPORATORS, ETC.

Gas Fitting, Roofing, Jobbing, and Tin Smithing done to Order.

E. P. WEBSTER & CO.,

DRUGGISTS & APOTHECARIES,

SIGN "GOLDEN MORTAR."

REID'S BLOCK, BAY STREET,

JACKSONVILLE, FLORIDA.

—:o:—

Persons, visiting Jacksonville, in need of pure Drugs and Medicines, fine Brandy, Wines, and other Liquors, Fancy Goods, Toilet Articles, fine Brushes, fine Soaps, fine Eau de Cologne, Florida Water, Rose Water, Orange-flower Water, Pomades, and every thing usually kept in a first-class Drug Store,—are invited to call, and look at our stock. The Compounding of Prescriptions made a Specialty. Satisfaction promised in all cases.

VISITORS
TO

Look out for the Golden Alligator,

AT

E. F. GILBERT'S
New Jewelry Establishment,

Where, in addition to the finest stock of

WATCHES, CLOCKS, JEWELRY, SILVER AND PLATED WARE,

They will find the best collection of

FLORIDA CURIOSITIES

in the State, at the LOWEST CASH PRICES, *comprising in part, Walking Canes, in every variety of beautiful native wood; Alligator Teeth, carved or gold mounted; Sea Beans, mounted in new and beautiful designs; Sea Shell Jewelry, Crosses, Card Baskets, etc., of exquisite workmanship; Plumes and Feathers of every hue; Corals, and hundreds of the Native Beauties of Florida. Monograms, and Fancy Engravings a specialty.*

Fine Watches and Chronometers repaired and rated. Remember GILBERT'S sign of the Golden Alligator, *Jacksonville, Florida.*

Charles L. Mather. Frank E. Little

C. L. MATHER & CO.,

Post Office Building, Jacksonville, Fla.

WHOLESALE AND RETAIL

STATIONERS,

BOOKSELLERS & NEWSDEALERS.

BOSTON, NEW YORK, PHILADELPHIA AND SAVANNAH DAILY PAPERS, *also all the latest* MAGAZINES AND PERIODICALS *constantly on hand.*

Parties visiting Florida can leave their subscriptions with us, for any length of time, and the same will be promptly forwarded to any point accessible by mail.

GUIDE BOOKS, RAILWAY GUIDES AND POCKET MAPS *in great variety.*

Call and examine our stock before purchasing elsewhere.

THE OLD RELIABLE
BROCK'S LINE OF STEAMERS,

RUNNING BETWEEN

Jacksonville and Enterprise,

ON THE

ST. JOHN'S RIVER, FLORIDA.

THE NEW AND ELEGANT PASSENGER STEAMER

FLORENCE

Leaves JACKSONVILLE daily (except Sundays) for PALATKA and all INTERMEDIATE POINTS, and connecting with Steamers for ENTERPRISE, CLAY SPRINGS, SALT LAKE, DUNN'S LAKE, and points on the OCKLAWAHA RIVER. At TOCOI with ST. JOHN'S RAILROAD for ST. AUGUSTINE, and returning to Jacksonville same evening in time to connect with all Northern Trains.

THE FAVORITE STEAMERS

"DARLINGTON" and "HATTIE"

Leave JACKSONVILLE on SUNDAYS and WEDNESDAYS at 9 a. m., RUNNING THROUGH TO ENTERPRISE, and stopping at all principal points on the River.

The Old Reputation of this Popular Line will be fully sustained, and every Comfort Guaranteed to its Patrons.

JACOB BROCK, Agent,

Jacksonville, Fla.

FOR ENTERPRISE, MELLONVILLE,

AND

All Landings on St. John's River.

THE
FAVORITE AND SPLENDID STEAMER,

Starlight,

Captain L. M. COXETTER,

LEAVES JACKSONVILLE EVERY

Tuesday & Friday for Enterprise

AND
ALL INTERMEDIATE LANDINGS on the St. JOHN'S RIVER.

The *Starlight* has recently been thoroughly overhauled, supplied with new boilers and refurnished, and is now in splendid order, offering the most agreeable means of reaching points on the

Upper St. John's, Indian and Oclawaha Rivers.

Her passenger accommodations are unsurpassed, and her table first-class.

Close communication made with the Charleston and Savannah Steamers. For full information apply to

GEO. R. FOSTER, Agent, Jacksonville.

HENRY A. L'ENGLE,

GRADUATED

PHARMACEUTIST,

Cor. Bay and Laura Streets,

JACKSONVILLE.

Go to the Corner of Bay and Laura Streets, where you will find a good stock of

PURE AND FRESH DRUGS

AND

CHEMICALS,

PATENT MEDICINES, PERFUMERY, TOILET ARTICLES,

FINE WINES AND LIQUORS,

FOR MEDICINAL PURPOSES.

Physician's Prescriptions accurately prepared at all hours of the day and night.

Clarendon House,

GREEN COVE SPRINGS, Fla.

ON THE

ST. JOHN'S RIVER,

30 Miles South of Jacksonville.

Daily Mail and two daily Steamers from Jacksonville to Green Cove.

Belonging to this house, and within 100 ft. of it, is the Green Cove Warm Sulphur Spring, discharging 3,000 gallons per minute, of temperature 78°.

This water is highly valuable in its medicinal qualities, in the following diseases. Rheumatism—Gout—Scrofula—Dyspepsia—Paralysis—Neuralgia—all Nervous Affections—Erysipelas, and all Eruptive Diseases—Kidney Disorders, and General Debility.

Large additions have been made, during the past season, to the Bathing facilities. The Baths and Dressing Rooms now occupy a space 200 ft. long by 50 ft. wide.

The house is supplied with water from the Spring, by means of water power.

HARRIS, APPLEGATE & CO., Proprietors.

The Union House,

AT

GREEN COVE SPRINGS,

30 MILES FROM JACKSONVILLE,

KEPT BY

MESSRS. REMINGTON & REED,

Is a most delightful place for visitors. They will find every comfort, and a fine table.

Mrs. FLEMING,

HIBERNIA, on the St. JOHN'S RIVER,

25 MILES ABOVE JACKSONVILLE,

PRIVATE BOARDING HOUSE.

A most delightful place for visitors from the North.

Palmetto House,

GREEN COVE SPRINGS,

FLORIDA.

THE CELEBRATED SULPHUR AND MINERAL SPRINGS

FOR

INVALIDS!

OPEN WINTER AND SUMMER.

WM. GRIFFITHS, Proprietor.

These Springs are situated thirty miles above Jacksonville; daily communication.

H. L. HART.   C. C. LYNDE.   S. L. MORRIS.

HART, LYNDE & Co., Proprietors.

The **Putnam House** has during the past Summer been put in thorough order, and an addition built containing forty comfortable rooms. The favorable reputation of the house will be maintained by the present proprietors, who promise nothing shall be left undone for the comfort of their guests.

HART, LYNDE & CO.

St. JOHN'S HOTEL,

PALATKA, East Florida.

P. & H. PETERMAN, Proprietors.

This Hotel is newly furnished throughout. A fine Billiard Room in connection with house, and guests will find everything for their comfort.

N. H. MORAGNE, M. D.,

WHOLESALE & RETAIL

DRUGGIST.

PALATKA, EAST FLORIDA.

JAMES BURT,

Real Estate Agent,

PALATKA, EAST FLORIDA.

FOR THE
Oclawaha River.

The fine Steamers of the Hart Line connect at Palatka with the Charleston and Savannah Steamers, leaving on their arrival

Sunday and Thursday Evenings.

These boats have been put in good order and a fine new steamer added to the line, so that passengers will find on board every comfort and a good table. By this route they visit the *most remarkable and most beautiful River of Florida*, the celebrated *Silver Spring*, and the noble *Lakes Harris and Eustace*.

Sportsmen will find game abundant on the whole route. For full information apply to

R. I. ADAMS, Agent.

Ocala House,

Situated six miles from Silver Springs, where a conveyance meets every boat on the Oclawaha River.

This house is pleasantly situated in the flourishing town of Ocala, encircled by pine groves, and acknowledged by the faculty as one of the most desirable winter resorts for invalids. Comfortable rooms and a good table furnished at moderate prices.

E. I. HARRIS, Proprietor.

BROCK HOUSE,

ENTERPRISE.

THE Brock House, beautifully situated on the shore of Lake Munroe, will be found by Invalids, Tourists and Sportsmen to combine every requisite for health, comfort, and enjoyment.

The rooms are large and comfortable, and the table excellent.

Splendid boating, fishing and hunting, in the immediate vicinity of the Hotel.

Arrangements can be here made for conveyances to Smyrna, Indian River, etc.

JACOB BROCK, Proprietor.

MELLONVILLE HOUSE,
MELLONVILLE.

This Hotel, commanding a splendid view of Lake Munroe, offers to the traveling public excellent accommodations at reasonable prices. Surrounded by Groves of Pines, its advantages for invalids cannot be surpassed.

Every facility for boating, hunting, fishing, and excursions to the Orange Groves and Mineral Springs of the neighborhood.

All Steamers on the St. John's stop at the Hotel landing, going and coming.

RAILROAD HOUSE,
TOCOI.

This House has been put in comfortable order, and is ready to receive permanent and transient visitors.

First-class beds and a "Cuisine," in every respect unexceptionable.

Meals furnished at any hour at short notice.

CHARLES THOMAS, Lessee.

FRONTING THE
PLAZA AND SEA WALL.

The St. Augustine Hotel, commanding a view of the bay and ocean, occupies the most desirable location in St. Augustine.

The reputation of the house as a first-class family hotel will be maintained by the present proprietors, and no effort be spared to provide every comfort to the traveler.

THE
Magnolia Hotel
ST. GEORGE STREET,
St. Augustine, Florida.

W. W. PALMER, - - - - Proprietor.
(*Late HOUGHTON & PALMER.*)

This favorite Hotel has been completely Renovated, internally and externally, and now presents unsurpassed accommodation for TOURISTS and INVALIDS. Single rooms and family apartments, *en suite*. The *cuisine* is in every respect unexceptionable. The Magnolia stands upon the highest ground in the city, and commands a fine view of the ocean

ORIENTAL HOUSE,

Charlotte St., North of Plaza,

St. AUGUSTINE, Fla.

On the European Plan,

$1 a day for occupying Room.

This Hotel is entirely newly furnished, is FIRST CLASS, and about two minutes' walk from Central Pier and Post Office. Restaurant for Ladies and Gentlemen attached to Hotel.

W. G. PONCE & Co., Proprietors.

T. A. PACETTI,

GRADUATED

PHARMACEUTIST,

St. Augustine Hotel,

St. AUGUSTINE, Fla.

Dealer in Drugs, Medicines, Perfumery, etc. Speciality—fine old Liquors, viz., Brandy, Whiskey, Wines, etc.; also, Cigars.

FLORIDA HOUSE,

St. AUGUSTINE.

THE Florida House, which all visitors to St. Augustine will remember, from its agreeable location and cheerful appearance—situated on St. George's Street, has undergone most important changes the past summer. A wing has been added on St. George's St., containing seventy large, well-ventilated and cheerful rooms, and the whole house has been renovated and refurnished throughout.

Guests will find the table in every way worthy of a first-class hotel, and the proprietor promises entire satisfaction to visitors.

The house will be heated throughout and gas and other conveniences furnished in every room.

I. H. REMER, Proprietor.

ANSLEY & BALLARD,

St. George St., St. Augustine,

DEALERS IN

WATCHES,

Jewelry, Clocks, Plated-Ware, Cutlery and Spectacles,

FANCY GOODS, STATIONERY,

AND

FLORIDA CURIOSITIES,

Sea Shells, Sea Beans, and Alligator Teeth,

HANDSOMELY CARVED and MOUNTED.

Corals, Bird Plumes, Feathers, Flowers, Palm Work, Coquina Ornaments and Walking Canes, in great variety.

St. GEORGE ST., St. Augustine, Fla.

D. J. LOPEZ,

DEALER IN

Drugs, Medicines, Chemicals,

Fine Toilet Soaps, Brushes, Combs, etc. Fancy Articles, Perfumery in great variety, and pure Wines and Liquors, for Medicinal Purposes only.

N. B.—Physicians, Prescriptions carefully Compounded. Foot of Central Wharf, opposite the St. Augustine Hotel.

St. AUGUSTINE, Fla.

B. GENOVAR,

WHOLESALE AND RETAIL DEALER IN

GROCERIES & PROVISIONS,

FURNITURE, HARDWARE,

WINES, LIQUORS,

Tobacco, Segars, Pipes, &c.

CHARLOTTE STREET, St. Augustine, E. Fla.

www.ingramcontent.com/pod-product-compliance
Lightning Source LLC
Chambersburg PA
CBHW021732220426
43662CB00008B/810